**14**

TURKEY

THE
MIDDLE
EAST

RUSSIA

CHINA

JAPAN

INDIA

THAILAND

PACIFIC
OCEAN

A

INDIAN OCEAN

AUSTRALIA

# The Usborne
# Little Round the World
# Cookbook

Angela Wilkes and Fiona Watt

Designed by Cristina Adami and Nelupa Hussain
Food photography: Howard Allman
Food stylist: Eliza Baird
Illustrated by Nadine Wickenden
Image manipulation: John Russell
Edited by Jenny Tyler
Managing designer: Mary Cartwright

# Contents

(v) suitable for vegetarians   * contains nuts

# Internet links

Look for the Internet links boxes that appear throughout this book. They contain descriptions of websites where you can find out more about a country, the type of food that is traditionally eaten or the ingredients.

To visit the websites, go to Usborne Quicklinks at **www.usborne-quicklinks.com** and enter the keywords "world cookbook". There, you will find links to all the sites described in this book and copies of the recipes that you can print out and keep.

Before using the Internet, please read the **Internet Safety Guidelines** and **Note for Parents** on page 94.

# Hints and tips

Before you try any recipe in this book, read it all the way through to make sure you have all the ingredients and equipment that you will need. Make sure you turn your oven on when the recipe tells you to, so that it will have heated up by the time you need to use it. You should be able to buy all the ingredients in a big supermarket, but if you live in a city you could also try specialist shops and ethnic markets.

**Put ingredients onto a clean chopping board before you cut them with a knife.**

## Cooking words

Here are some of the cooking words which are used in the book. If you come across a word in a recipe which you don't understand, remember to turn back to these pages.

### For how many?

Most of the recipes in this book are enough for four people unless the recipe says otherwise.

### Simmering

Cooking something liquid over a low heat so that it bubbles gently, but does not boil.

### Sifting

Shake flour or sugar through a sieve to get rid of lumps and make it light and airy.

### Beating

Stir as hard as you can with a wooden spoon until the mixture is pale and creamy.

### Whisking

Move a whisk around and around, very quickly. Hold the bowl with one hand as you do it.

### Chopping an onion

1. Cut the onion in half. Lay each half, cut-side down onto a chopping board and make cuts across it.

2. Then, turn the onion and cut across the first cuts at right angles, so that you chop it into small pieces.

### Making stock

1. Boil some water in a kettle. Either cut up or crumble a stock cube and put it into a measuring jug.

2. Pour in the amount of boiling water you need for your recipe. Stir well until the stock cube dissolves completely.

4

## Weighing and measuring

Weigh the dry ingredients on kitchen scales and measure the liquid ones in a measuring jug.

### Grams or ounces?

The ingredients are given in grams and ounces. Use one set or the other, don't swap them around.

## A spoonful

In this book, a "spoonful" means a level spoonful.

## A pinch

A "pinch" means the amount you can pinch between your thumb and your forefinger.

## Using a cooker

When you put things into an oven to cook, put them onto the middle shelf, unless the recipe says something different. Move the shelves to the right position before you switch on the oven.

## Fan ovens

If you have a fan oven, you will need to turn it to a lower temperature than the one shown in this book. Follow the instructions in the oven's manual.

# Be safe

✻ Whenever you find it difficult to do something, ask someone to help you.

✻ Be very careful when you are slicing things with a sharp knife. Always put the ingredients onto a chopping board.

✻ Always put on oven gloves before picking up anything hot or when putting things into or taking them out of the oven.

✻ Don't leave the kitchen while electric or gas rings are on.

✻ If you spill something on the floor, wipe it up at once in case you slip on it.

✻ When you have finished cooking, put everything away and clean up any mess and leave the kitchen tidy.

## Kneading

1. Use the heels of both hands or your knuckles to push a ball of dough away from you.

2. Fold the dough in half and turn it around. Push it away from you, as you did in step 1.

3. Carry on folding, turning and pushing until the dough feels smooth and stretchy.

## Rubbing in

Mix butter and flour by rubbing them with your fingertips until they look like breadcrumbs.

## Separating an egg

1. Gently crack the egg on the edge of a bowl to break the shell. Pull the shell apart, keeping the egg in one half.

2. Tip the yolk from one half to the other, so that the white slips into the bowl. Put the yolk in another bowl.

## Folding in

Mix two things together by slicing into the mixture and gently turning it over and over until it is evenly mixed.

## Greasing

Rub a baking tin or oven-proof dish with butter, oil or margarine on kitchen paper. This stops food from sticking.

5

# The United States of America

The United States of America is an enormous country made up of 50 different states. Because it is so big, there is a huge variety of different landscapes ranging from hot deserts to huge mountains, rolling grasslands to wooded hills. Over the last 300 years people have come to live in the United States from all over the world, bringing with them customs and recipes.

**This is the Statue of Liberty. It stands on Liberty Island, overlooking the harbour of New York.**

## New York cheesecake

This delicious creamy cheesecake is based on a traditional Jewish recipe. You have to allow time for it to chill, so it is best to make it the day before you want to eat it. You will need a 20cm (8in.) springform cake tin.

175g/6oz. digestive
  biscuits
85g/3oz. butter
3 eggs
340g/12oz. cream
  cheese or curd cheese
85g/3oz. caster sugar
150ml/1⁄4 pint
  double cream
juice of 1 lemon
1 tablespoon cornflour

Oven temperature:
150°C/300°F/Gas mark 2

1. Break the digestive biscuits into a big plastic bag. Roll a rolling pin over the bag to crush the biscuits into crumbs.

2. Melt the butter in a pan over a low heat. Turn off the heat, then stir the biscuit crumbs into the butter.

3. Turn on the oven. Grease the cake tin. Tip the biscuit crumbs into it and press them down firmly with a spoon.

4. Bake the biscuit base for 20 minutes. Meanwhile, separate the eggs into two different bowls.

5. Beat together the cheese and egg yolks. Stir in the sugar, cream, lemon juice and cornflour. Mix them well.

Delicatessens, like this one in Times Square, New York, are common in large cities in America. As well as selling sandwiches and snacks, they also sell fruit and vegetables.

# New York delis

New York is famous for its delicatessens. These are small food shops where you can buy sandwiches, salads, cold meats and other tasty snacks. Many of the delis specialize in particular types of food, such as Italian or Jewish food.

## Internet links

Go to **www.usborne-quicklinks.com** and enter the keywords "world cookbook" for links to the following websites:

**Website 1** Find a recipe from each of the 50 states in America.

**Website 2** See live images from Times Square in New York.

6. Then, in a separate bowl, whisk the egg whites until they are firm and form peaks. It may take some time.

7. Add them to the cheese mixture. Turn them over gently with a metal spoon until they are mixed in.

8. Pour the mixture onto the biscuit base and smooth it level. Then, put it in the oven and bake it for 50-55 minutes.

9. Turn off the oven, but leave the cheesecake to cool inside it. This will stop the top of the cheesecake from cracking.

If you want to decorate the top of your cheesecake, sprinkle it with finely-grated lemon peel or some icing sugar.

United States of America

# Chocolate brownies

Chocolate brownies are American cakes. They are crisp and crunchy on the top and slightly gooey in the middle. Traditionally they are made with walnuts or pecan nuts, but leave them out if you can't eat nuts, or replace them with the same quantity of raisins.

175g/6oz. walnuts or pecan nuts
115g/4oz. plain chocolate
175g/6oz. butter
340g/12oz. caster sugar
1 teaspoon vanilla essence
3 eggs
115g/4oz. plain flour
1 level teaspoon baking powder

A baking tin 22x30cm (9x12in.) and 2.5cm (1in.) deep

Oven temperature: 180°C/ 350°F/Gas mark 4

1. Grease the baking tin. Put it onto baking parchment. Draw around the tin, cut out the shape and put it in the bottom.

2. Turn on the oven. Put the nuts into a clean plastic bag and roll a rolling pin over them to break them into pieces.

3. Break the chocolate into pieces and put it into a heat-proof bowl. Stand the bowl over a pan of simmering water.

4. Cut the butter into pieces and add it to the bowl. Stir the butter and the chocolate until they melt.

5. Pour the melted chocolate and butter into a mixing bowl. Stir in the caster sugar and vanilla essence.

6. Whisk the eggs in another bowl. Beat them into the chocolate mixture bit by bit, using a wooden spoon.

7. Sift the flour and baking powder into the bowl and add the pieces of nut. Mix everything together well.

8. Pour the mixture into the baking tin and smooth the top of it with a knife. Bake it for about 40 minutes.

9. Let the mixture cool a little, then cut the brownies into squares. Leave them on a wire rack to cool.

**Use either walnuts or pecan nuts, and plain chocolate, to make brownies.**

Brownies are best
eaten the day you make
them, but they will keep for a day
or so in an airtight container.

# Pumpkin pie

A traditional sweet dish in
America is pumpkin pie. It
is eaten on Thanksgiving Day,
a national holiday. Mashed
or puréed pumpkin is mixed
with eggs and cream and
baked in a pastry pie. Roast,
baked and boiled pumpkin
is also eaten at other times.

Pumpkins, like squashes (see
page 26), grow on long 'vines'.

# Canada

Canada is the second largest country in the world, but has a small population. Most Canadians live in the south, near the border with the United States. Canada has many different types of landscape such as vast fields of wheat, mountains and huge lakes. Canadian food is similar to food in the United States. It also has strong European influences, because of the many British and French people who moved there.

Serve the pancakes hot with maple syrup poured on top.

## Tapping for syrup

Maple syrup comes from the sap of maple trees. Tubes are drilled into the trunk and the sap slowly drips out. This is called 'tapping' the tree. The sap is then boiled to make maple syrup.

The sap is collected as it drips from tubes pushed into the trunk of a maple tree.

These are maple leaves. A maple leaf is the national emblem of Canada.

### Internet link

Go to **www.usborne-quicklinks.com** and enter the keywords "world cookbook" for a link to a website where you can find out more about maple syrup, and Canada's history.

# Canadian pancakes

Canadian pancakes are small and puffy with crisp edges. In Canada, people often eat them for breakfast.

**These mountains are part of a high mountain range called the Rockies, which lies along the west coast of Canada.**

For 8-10 pancakes

145g/5oz. plain flour
2 teaspoons baking
   powder
a pinch of salt
1 egg
4 tablespoons vegetable
   oil
300ml/½ pint milk
maple syrup

1. Sift the flour, baking powder and salt into a mixing bowl, then use a spoon to make a well in the middle.

2. Carefully break the egg into another bowl. Whisk it with two tablespoons of the oil and the milk.

3. Beat the egg mixture into the flour, a little at a time, until everything is mixed and makes a smooth batter.

4. Pour the remaining two tablespoons of oil into a frying pan and heat it until a faint haze rises from the pan.

5. Carefully spoon two tablespoons of batter into the pan to make one pancake. Add batter to make two more.

6. Cook the pancakes for about a minute on one side. When they begin to bubble, turn them over with a spatula.

7. Cook the pancakes for another minute, until they puff up. Lift them out of the pan onto a warm plate.

# Latin America

Latin America is the name given to Mexico and all the countries in Central and South America. The people are descended from tribes of Indians, but Spanish is the main language except in Brazil, where people speak Portuguese. Latin America has some of the largest rainforests in the world. It also has high mountains and huge grasslands, called the Pampas. Latin American food is hot and spicy. The main ingredients are tomatoes, chilli peppers, corn and beans.

If you go to a food market in Mexico, you will see people cooking the local dishes. These tortillas, being cooked on a hot plate, will be filled with hot chilli sauce from the pans.

## Tacos

Tacos are crisp corn pancakes filled with a spicy meat mixture. Delicious toppings, such as guacamole, refried beans or tomato salsa are then added. You can buy taco shells at large supermarkets. Turn over the page to find out how to make guacamole, refried beans and tomato salsa.

1 medium onion
1 clove of garlic
a small lettuce
4 tomatoes
2 tablespoons
    vegetable oil
8 taco shells

450g/1lb. minced beef
1 teaspoon cinnamon
a pinch mild chilli pepper
a pinch salt and black
    pepper
soured cream

Oven temperature:
180°C/350°F/Gas mark 4

1. Turn on the oven. Peel and chop the onion. Peel and crush the garlic. Cut the lettuce into strips and slice the tomatoes.

2. Heat the vegetable oil in a large pan. Cook the onion and garlic over a low heat until they are soft.

3. Turn up the heat. Add the meat to the pan. Cook it, stirring it all the time, until it is brown all over.

4. Add the cinnamon, chilli pepper, salt and pepper, then cook it over a low heat for about ten minutes.

5. Stand the tacos on a baking sheet. Put them in the oven for three minutes so that they warm up.

6. Spoon some of the meat into each taco and add lettuce, tomato and a tablespoon of soured cream on top.

## Internet link

Go to **www.usborne-quicklinks.com** and enter the keywords "world cookbook" for a link to a website to find out how food plays a central part in Mexico's ancient festival, the Days of the Dead, and try some traditional recipes.

**Serve the tacos with bowls of guacamole, salsa and refried beans, so that people can help themselves to the toppings.**

Guacamole

Refried beans

Tomato salsa

## Latin America

# Guacamole

Serve this creamy avocado dip with tacos. You will need really ripe avocados, which are soft when you press them.

2 ripe avocados
200g/7oz. can chopped
  tomatoes, drained
juice of half a lemon
a few drops of chilli sauce
a pinch of salt and
  of black pepper

1. Cut each avocado in half lengthways around the stone. Scoop the stone out of the middle with a spoon.

2. Use the spoon to scoop the avocado flesh into a bowl. Then, mash it into a smooth, thick paste with a fork.

3. Mix all the other ingredients into the mashed avocado and beat the mixture until smooth and creamy.

# Tomato salsa

In Latin America, people serve fresh, spicy sauces called salsas with many dishes, including tacos. Some of the salsas are made with fresh chillies which are so hot they make your mouth burn. For this recipe, allow time for the salsa to stand for about an hour after you have made it. This brings out its full flavour.

**Habañero chillies are the hottest chillies you can get.**

**Jalapeño chillies are quite hot. They are traditionally used in salsas.**

4 ripe, tasty tomatoes
1 small red onion
6 sprigs of fresh
  coriander
A few drops of chilli
  sauce
salt and black pepper

1. Put the tomatoes into a bowl of boiling water for two minutes, then a bowl of cold water for two minutes.

2. Slip the skins off the tomatoes, then chop them finely. Cut the ends off the onion and peel it, then chop it finely.

3. Chop the coriander. Then, mix all the ingredients together in a bowl, then leave it to stand for an hour.

# Refried beans

Latin American cooks use beans in lots of different ways. Here, they are made into a dish to serve with tacos.

1 medium onion
1 clove garlic
1 tablespoon vegetable oil

400g/14oz. can red kidney beans
a pinch of salt and of black pepper

1. Peel the onion and chop it finely. Peel the clove of garlic and crush it with a fork or in a garlic press.

2. Heat the oil in a frying pan until a haze rises. Cook the onion and garlic over a low heat until soft.

3. Drain the beans in a sieve, then add them to the pan. Mash them into the onions and garlic with a fork.

4. Fry the bean mixture until it is hot all the way through. Stir it to stop it from sticking. Add the salt and pepper.

5. Spoon the mixture into a bowl. Sprinkle it with grated cheese, or add it to tacos (see pages 12-13).

## Bean feast

Mexican cooks use red kidney beans in lots of their recipes, particularly in hot, spicy stews. Black beans are popular all over Latin America. You can use most sorts of beans to make refried beans.

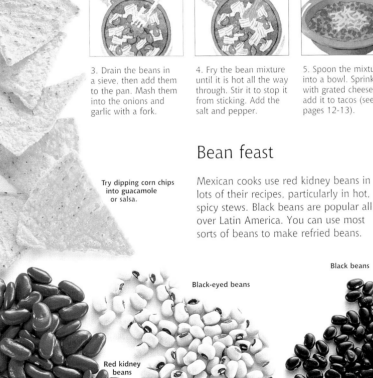

Try dipping corn chips into guacamole or salsa.

Black beans

Black-eyed beans

Red kidney beans

# Fruit around the world

Many shops and large supermarkets sell a huge variety of fruit from different countries around the world. Many of them look strange and have unusual names, but they are all worth trying as many of them taste quite delicious and different from anything you may have eaten before.

## Internet link

Go to **www.usborne-quicklinks.com** and enter the keywords "world cookbook" for a link to a website where you can find out about different fruits, such as rambutan, tamarind or breadfruit.

**Guava -** has a delicate, refreshing taste. It is ripe when it is slightly soft. You don't need to peel it, but don't eat the seeds.

**Pawpaw (papaya) -** a sweet, juicy fruit which is ripe when it's slightly soft. Cut it in half and scoop out the seeds. Don't eat the skin or the seeds.

**Passion fruit -** ripe when its skin is dark and wrinkled. Cut it in half and scoop out the juicy flesh and seeds.

**Pomegranate -** pink, juicy and sweet with lots of seeds. To eat a pomegranate, cut it in half and scoop out the seeds. You don't eat the skin.

**Sharon fruit (persimmon) -** looks a little like a tomato. It is ripe when soft, and taste is very sweet. You can eat it whole or scoop out the flesh.

16

**Star fruit (carambola) -** have a delicate, but sharp flavour. They are ripe when the edges are slightly brown.

**Pineapple -** cut off the skin and cut out the core, then slice the flesh. If ripe, it should smell sweet, but not too strongly.

**Kumquats -** taste a little bit sour. Eat them whole without peeling them.

**Tamarillo -** a red fruit with a bitter taste. It can be eaten raw or cooked. They are ripe when slightly soft.

**Physalis -** a slightly bitter fruit, ripe when it is soft. Pull back the papery leaves and eat the whole berry.

**Mangosteen -** slice through the thick skin, pull the halves apart and scoop out the sweet flesh. Ripe when the skin is dark purple.

**Lychees (litchi) -** sweet and juicy, they are ripe when soft. Peel off the skin and eat the white fruit.

**Mango -** a very sweet fruit. It is ripe when slightly soft. Page 19 shows you how to cut one open.

**Kiwi fruit -** peel off the skin and slice it, or cut the top off and scoop out the inside.

**Horned melon (kiwano) -** tastes a little like cucumber. Cut it in half and eat the seeds inside.

# The Caribbean

The Caribbean, or the West Indies as it is often known, is made up of hundreds of tropical islands. They are famous for their clear blue seas, hot sun, white sands and coral reefs. The islands lie in the Caribbean Sea, forming an arc from the Gulf of Mexico down to Venezuela in South America. There are 25 separate countries. Over the centuries, many different peoples have settled in the Caribbean, bringing their own traditions with them. Caribbean cooking is exotic and spicy, an exciting mixture of African, Asian and European cooking, based on fresh seafood, chicken, rice, beans and tropical fruits.

Nowhere in the Caribbean is far from the sea, so fresh fish is the main ingredient of many dishes.

Tall coconut palm trees, like these, grow on all the islands in the Caribbean.

## Mango fool

This fruit fool makes a delicious pudding. It is important to use ripe mangoes. They should have a strong scent and should "give" a little when you press them lightly.

2 ripe mangoes
1 lemon or lime
150ml/¼ pint whipping cream
145g/5oz. thick, natural yogurt

4-5 dessertspoons coconut milk (If you don't like coconut or you are allergic to it, leave it out.)

Fresh and dried coconut, as well as coconut milk are important ingredients in Caribbean cooking.

1. Put the mangoes onto a chopping board and slice them lengthways, either side of the big stone in the middle.

2. Make cuts along and across the flesh, as shown then slice the chunks of mango away from the skin.

3. Put the mango flesh into a blender and liquidize it, or put it in a bowl and mash it with a fork.

4. Cut the lemon or lime in half and squeeze out the juice. Stir the juice into the mango purée and mix well.

5. In another bowl, whisk the cream until it starts to thicken, but don't whisk it so much that it forms peaks.

6. Stir the yogurt and the coconut milk into the mango. Then, gently fold in the cream so that everything is mixed.

## Internet link

Go to **www.usborne-quicklinks.com** and enter the keywords "world cookbook" for a link to a website where you can search through a list of different things to eat in the Caribbean.

**Pour the fool into bowls or glasses and put them into a refrigerator to chill. You could decorate them with slices of mango before serving.**

# Banana bread

People eat and cook bananas in many different ways in the Caribbean. They are eaten fresh, baked, boiled and fried. In this recipe, they are made into scrumptious, moist banana bread. This is a tea bread, more like a cake in some ways than bread. It is best eaten buttered, while still slightly warm.

115g/4oz. softened butter
85g/3oz. caster sugar
85g/3oz. soft brown sugar
2 tablespoons milk
a pinch of salt
2 teaspoons baking powder
a pinch of ground nutmeg
85g/3oz. raisins
1 egg

85g/3oz. chopped walnuts
225g/8oz. wholemeal flour
2 large bananas
1 teaspoon vanilla essence or extract

a 600ml/1pint loaf tin

Oven temperature:
180°C/350°F/Gas mark 4

1. Turn on the oven. Lightly grease the loaf tin with butter and line its base with a piece of baking parchment.

2. Cut the butter into cubes and put them into a bowl. Add both types of sugar and beat well with a wooden spoon.

These slices of banana bread are sitting on a fresh banana leaf. The leaves can grow up to 4m (13ft.) in length.

3. Carry on beating the butter and sugar together with the spoon until the mixture is pale, soft and creamy.

4. Sift the flour, salt, baking powder and nutmeg into another bowl. Add the raisins and walnuts.

5. Beat the egg and milk together in a cup. Beat them into the butter and sugar mixture, a little at a time.

6. Fold the flour mixture gently into the butter mixture, with a metal spoon, until everything is mixed well.

7. Peel the bananas. Put them in a bowl and mash them with a fork. Add the vanilla essence or extract and stir it in.

8. Stir the mashed banana into the cake mixture, then pour it into the loaf tin. Use a knife to smooth the top.

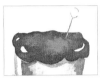

9. Bake the banana bread for one hour, or until a skewer comes out clean when you push it into the loaf.

10. Let the bread cool in the tin for five minutes, then turn it out onto a wire rack to finish cooling.

# Harvesting bananas

Bananas grow in warm tropical countries. They are picked while they are still green so that they ripen by the time they are sold. There are hundreds of different types, such as red bananas and Manzanos, which are small, stubby bananas that taste like apples. In the Caribbean, large green bananas, called plantains, are cooked and eaten as a vegetable (see page 27).

**While bananas are growing, they are covered with a bag to protect them from the wind and from damage by insects and bats.**

# Africa

Africa is a huge continent, with over fifty countries. The landscape ranges from tropical rainforests to deserts, vast grasslands and high mountains. Each country is home to many different peoples, all with their own traditions. African food is based on the crops which grow locally. Groundnuts, cassava, yams and bananas grow in tropical regions. Corn and wheat are grown in drier areas.

## Internet link

Go to **www.usborne-quicklinks.com** and enter the keywords "world cookbook" for a link to a website where you can learn more about Africa and try some African recipes.

## Bobotie

Bobotie is a traditional dish from South Africa which makes a filling main course. Its unusual combination of ingredients, including nuts and curry powder, turns minced beef into a tasty dish.

1 onion
1 clove garlic
55g/2oz. dried apricots
2 slices white bread
300ml/½ pint milk
30g/1oz. butter
450g/1lb. minced beef
1 teaspoon mild curry powder
half a teaspoon chilli powder

2 tablespoons lemon juice
salt and black pepper
55g/2oz. raisins
55g/2oz. flaked almonds
2 eggs

a large, greased ovenproof dish

Oven temperature:
180°C/350°F/Gas mark 4

Bobotie has an eggy mixture poured on top. It sets and turns golden when it is cooked. Serve the bobotie hot, straight from the oven.

1. Peel the onion and chop it finely. Peel and crush the clove of garlic. Chop the dried apricots finely.

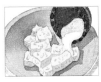

2. Tear the bread into pieces. Put it into a shallow bowl and pour half the milk over it. Leave it to soak.

3. Melt the butter in a frying pan. Cook the onion and garlic over a low heat for five minutes, until they are soft.

4. Add the minced beef. Cook it for another five minutes, stirring it all the time, until it is brown all over.

5. Mix the curry powder, chilli powder, lemon juice, and a pinch of salt and pepper in a bowl. Add the meat mixture.

6. Add the raisins, almonds, apricots and soaked bread. Stir in the remaining milk that the bread was soaked in.

7. Spoon the mixture into the greased dish. Whisk the eggs and the rest of the milk together. Pour it over the meat.

8. Put the dish into the oven and bake it for 45-50 minutes, until the topping has set and turned golden.

# Village life

Most Africans live in the countryside, often in tribal villages. They usually grow their own food and cook traditional dishes. Droughts or heavy rain sometimes ruin their crops and people don't have enough to eat.

An Ethiopian woman, cooking injera, a type of flat bread. It is often eaten with wat, a spicy stew made with meat, fish or vegetables.

# Africa

# Peanut bread

Peanuts are known as groundnuts in Africa and are one of the main crops grown. This recipe uses chopped peanuts to make a type of heavy bread.

55g/2oz. unsalted, shelled peanuts
340g/12oz. plain flour
a pinch of salt
3 teaspoons baking powder
1 egg
300ml/½ pint milk

30g/1oz. caster sugar

A baking tray 18x28cm (7x11in.) and 4cm (1½ in.) deep

Oven temperature:
180°C/350°F/Gas mark 4

1. Put a little butter or oil onto some kitchen paper and rub it lightly over the bottom and sides of the baking tray.

2. Put the peanuts into a clean plastic bag and roll a rolling pin over them, or put them into a blender to chop them.

3. Sift the flour, salt and baking powder into a large mixing bowl. Break the egg into a cup and beat it with a fork.

4. Add the milk, sugar, beaten egg and chopped peanuts to the flour. Mix everything together well.

5. Spoon the mixture into the baking tray. Smooth the top and then leave it for 20 minutes to settle.

6. Bake the bread for 45-50 minutes, until the top is golden brown. Let it cool a little, then cut it into squares.

7. Use a fish slice or a spatula to lift the squares onto a wire rack. Leave them to cool completely.

**The peanut bread will keep for several days if you store it in an airtight container.**

If you can only get peanuts in their shells, twist the shell to break them open. There are usually two peanuts in each shell.

# African grains

In Africa, people eat a lot of grains and root vegetables. In many places, they grind maize or corn and then cook it to make a thick kind of porridge called "mealie meal". They also grind dried cassava roots into a type of flour to make bread and dumplings.

# Groundnut paste

In West Africa, people use groundnut paste for cooking. It is smooth and buttery, rather like peanut butter. They use it to make soups and add it to chicken or vegetables.

**In countries such as Burkina Faso in West Africa, corn is pounded with wooden poles to make flour.**

# Vegetables around the world

Vegetables vary around the world, depending on the climate. All vegetables come from different parts of plants. Some are roots, others are shoots, pods or leaves. Big supermarkets usually have a wide selection of vegetables. Other good places to look are specialist shops, or street markets in big cities.

**Cassava -** a root vegetable, eaten mainly in tropical areas. It is peeled then the white flesh is boiled, fried, or made into flour.

**Kohlrabi -** tastes like a sweet turnip. Peel it, then cut it into chunks and steam or boil it.

**Avocado -** actually a fruit, but is eaten as a vegetable. It is ripe if it is slightly soft. Cut it in half, pull it apart, remove the stone and peel off the skin.

**Squashes -** there are many types of squash. They are often stuffed and baked, or boiled and then mashed. Each type of squash has its own delicate flavour.

**Fennel** - tastes like aniseed. Cut away any damaged outer leaves and slice it thinly. Use it raw in salads, or cooked.

**Acorn squash**

**Chicory -** crisp white leaves with a slightly bitter taste. Cut off a slice at the root end, then rinse the leaves. It can be used raw in salads, or cooked.

**Pak-choi (bok choy) -** a Chinese cabbage with dark green leaves and juicy stems. The stalks and leaves are usually chopped and stir-fried. It is used a lot in Chinese cooking.

**Butternut squash**

**Spaghetti squash**

**Plantain -** a type of banana, but bigger and less sweet. It is eaten as a vegetable and used in savoury dishes, especially in the Caribbean and Africa.

**Sweet potato -** a root vegetable. Usually baked, mashed or roasted. It is confusingly known as a yam in the United States (see below).

**Okra (ladies' fingers) -** Trim off the stalks and cook gently in butter or oil. They are eaten as a vegetable or cooked in stews.

**Mangetout (snow peas) -** tender pea pods which are eaten whole. Trim off their stalk and tail. Eat them raw in salads, or steam them so they are still slightly crunchy.

**Yam -** popular in Africa, South and Central America, and the Caribbean. It is peeled, then boiled or baked and mashed with spices, or cooked like potatoes.

**Asparagus -** can be green or white and has a delicate flavour. It is steamed or boiled and served hot with a butter sauce as a starter, or cold with salad dressing.

## Internet links

Go to **www.usborne-quicklinks.com** and enter the keywords "world cookbook" for links to the following websites:

**Website 1**  Find out about cooking cassava.

**Website 2**  See different kinds of squashes.

**Website 3**  Facts and pictures about potatoes.

# France

France is famous for its delicious food and cooking. Each region has its own specialities based on food that is produced there. Normandy, in Northern France, is the main apple-growing area of the country and is dotted with orchards. The region is also famous for its dairy products, such as butter, cream, and cheese, such as Camembert. Other regions also have traditional dishes. For example, Quiche Lorraine, a pastry dish filled with eggs, cream and bacon, is named after the Lorraine region in Eastern France.

## French apple tart

In France, you can buy fruit tarts, pastries and cakes at pastry shops called pâtisseries. Each region has its own special tarts - this one comes from Normandy.

**Garlic and onions are both common ingredients in French cooking. You will see them displayed like this in markets all over France.**

### Internet links

Go to **www.usborne-quicklinks.com** and enter the keywords "world cookbook" for links to the following websites:

**Website 1** Find out about the kinds of things eaten everyday in France.

**Website 2** See a translation of a French menu.

| | |
|---|---|
| 175g/6oz. plain flour | 3 eating apples |
| 85g/3oz. chilled butter | 2 tablespoons apricot jam |
| 30g/1oz. caster sugar | 2 tablespoons hot water |
| 1 egg yolk, beaten | |
| 1-2 tablespoons cold water | a 20cm (8in.) flan dish |
| 450g/1lb. cooking apples | Oven temperature: |
| 55g/2oz. caster sugar | 200°C/400°F/Gas mark 6 |

**Orchards, like this, growing apples and pears are found all over Normandy.**

1. Sift the flour into a large mixing bowl. Cut the butter into small pieces and add them to the flour.

2. Rub the butter into the flour with your fingers until the mixture looks like breadcrumbs. Add 30g/1oz. caster sugar.

3. Mix in the beaten egg yolk and enough water to make a ball of dough. Put it into a refrigerator for 30 minutes.

4. Turn on the oven. Peel the cooking apples. cut them into quarters and cut out the cores. Slice the quarters.

5. Put the apples, cold water and sugar into a saucepan. Cook them over a low heat until the apple is soft. Stir well.

6. Sprinkle some flour onto a board and onto a rolling pin. Roll the pastry into a big circle about 2cm/1in. thick.

7. Line the flan dish with the pastry. Prick it with a fork and trim the edges with a knife. Bake it for ten minutes.

8. Spoon the cooked apple into the pastry case. Slice the eating apples and arrange them in circles on top.

9. Mix the jam with the hot water and brush it over the sliced apples to glaze them. Bake the tart for 30 minutes.

**Serve slices of the tart hot or cold, with a spoonful of whipped cream.**

# Salade niçoise

This is a delicious tuna salad which was first made in Nice in the South of France, so its name means "salad from Nice". It includes local ingredients, such as tomatoes, anchovies and juicy black olives. Eat the salad with fresh French bread.

450g/1lb. new potatoes
2 eggs
115g/4oz. French beans
6 tomatoes
1 can anchovies
1 crisp lettuce
3 tablespoons of olive oil

1 dessertspoon wine vinegar
½ teaspoon French mustard
a pinch of salt and pepper
400g/14oz. can of tuna
50g/2oz. pitted black olives

**Try filling a roll or piece of bread with the salade niçoise ingredients.**

1. Scrub the potatoes. Cook them in boiling water for 15 minutes until tender. Drain them and let them cool.

2. Boil the eggs for ten minutes. Put them in a bowl of cold water to let them cool. Tap them and peel off the shells.

3. Trim the ends off the beans. Cook them in boiling water for five minutes. Rinse them with cold water.

4. Cut the tomatoes into quarters. Slice the potatoes. Drain the anchovies and cut them in half lengthwise.

5. Wash the lettuce leaves in cold water. Pat them dry and arrange them in the bottom of a large salad bowl.

6. Put the potatoes on top of the lettuce. Drain the tuna and put it on top. Add the beans, tomatoes and anchovies.

7. For the dressing, put the olive oil, vinegar, mustard, salt and pepper into a jar. Screw on the lid and shake really well.

8. Drizzle on the dressing. Slice the hard-boiled eggs and put them into the bowl, along with the olives.

# Markets

Every region in France has its own style of cooking. If you visit a market you may spot the kinds of ingredients which are included in many of the recipes which come from that area. For example, in Brittany in the north-west of France, you'll find lots of different kinds of seafood, and in the Alps, you'll see delicious French cheeses.

**This is a typical French fruit and vegetable market in Gers, France.**

# Spain

Spain is a country of contrasts - from the mountains and hills of the north to the sun-baked plains and beaches in the south. Spanish cooking has been influenced by the Arabs who lived there for over a thousand years, and by Spain's great explorers who brought back ingredients from their journeys.

The area around Seville in southern Spain is famous for orange trees.

## Internet link

Go to **www.usborne-quicklinks.com** and enter the keywords "world cookbook" for a link to a website where you can discover more about traditional Spanish food.

## Saffron

Saffron is the most expensive spice in the world. The threads are the stamens of purple autumn crocuses which grow in Spain. The name saffron, comes from the Arabic word "za'fran", which means yellow. It is used in cooking to colour and flavour dishes.

The stamens are picked by hand, which is why saffron costs so much.

## Paella

Paella is Spain's most famous dish. Rice is slowly cooked with chicken, seafood and saffron to create a filling meal. To make paella, you will need a large frying pan with a lid.

1 medium onion
1 red pepper
6 tomatoes
a clove of garlic
2 skinned chicken breasts
2 tablespoons olive oil
1 chicken stock cube
450ml/¾ pint boiling water
225g/8oz. paella or risotto rice
1 teaspoon saffron threads
a pinch of salt and of black pepper
115g/4oz. peeled prawns
55g/2oz. frozen peas
6 fresh mussels

1. Chop the onion finely. Core and slice the red pepper. Chop the tomatoes. Peel and crush the clove of garlic.

2. Cut the chicken into narrow strips. Heat the oil in the frying pan, then fry the chicken until it is golden brown.

3. Remove the chicken from the pan. Fry the red pepper, onion and garlic over a low heat until soft. Add the tomatoes.

4. Make the stock in a jug (see page 4). Pour the stock into the pan. Stir in the rice, chicken, saffron, salt and pepper.

5. Put the lid on the frying pan and cook the paella over a low heat for about 15 minutes, stirring occasionally.

6. Stir in the prawns and peas. Arrange the mussels on top, then cook the paella for five more minutes.

The paella is ready when the rice is tender and the mussels have opened. If any mussels don't open when you cook them, throw them away - don't try to eat them.

# Fish and seafood

**Swordfish**

**Salmon**

**Tuna**

**Fish steaks -** many large fish, such as tuna, are cut into pieces, known as steaks before they are cooked. They are often baked with a sauce.

All around the world, fish and seafood are one of the main ingredients in regions near the sea. If you visit a fish market you'll see the type of fish which are caught locally. Fish are prepared in lots of different ways, such as grilled or fried. In some countries they are dried or preserved in salt.

**Langoustine (Dublin Bay prawn) -** break off the tail and pull it apart to get at the delicious white flesh inside.

**Prawns -** shellfish with a delicate flavour and firm flesh. They turn orange when they are cooked.

**Mussels -** tasty shellfish which are sold fresh in their shells. When cooked, the shells open to reveal the flesh inside.

**Lemon sole -** a flat fish with a light flavour and texture. It is cooked whole or cut into boneless "fillets".

**Crab -** there are lots of different types of crab around the world. They are boiled, then the shell is cracked open to remove the flesh.

**Red snapper -** has tasty white flesh. It is often grilled, baked whole, steamed or fried. Large snapper are cut into steaks.

**Sea bass -** a delicately-flavoured fish, which is often roasted or steamed.

**Sardines -** a rich-flavoured fish. Fresh sardines are often grilled, or barbecued. They are popular in Mediterranean countries, especially Portugal.

**Mackerel -** has a strong flavour and is quite rich. It is usually grilled, barbecued or baked.

**Trout -** a freshwater fish which is usually cooked whole. It is baked, grilled or fried.

**Dorade -** a tasty fish with a firm texture, which is usually baked or grilled.

**Whitebait -** tiny fish which are eaten whole. They are usually coated with flour and fried.

**Clams -** prepared and eaten in the same way as mussels. In Italy they are eaten with pasta and in America they are used in a seafood soup called a clam chowder.

## Internet link

Go to **www.usborne-quicklinks.com** and enter the keywords "world cookbook" for a link to a website where you can search an extensive database and find out where different species of fish come from and how they live.

# Italy

Italy is famous for its cooking, especially its pasta, pizzas and ice cream. There is an enormous variety of dishes, each based on the fresh food produced locally. As in France, each region has its own specialities.

In Italy, fresh pasta is often sold loose by weight, as in this pasta shop in Bologna.

**Spaghetti**

There are hundreds of different shapes of pasta. They are usually served with sauces or stuffed with a filling. Green pasta is made with spinach.

**Lasagne**

## Internet link

Go to **www.usborne-quicklinks.com** and enter the keywords "world cookbook" for a link to a website where you can find out the names of lots of different shapes of pasta.

If you see the word 'rigate' on a packet of pasta, it just means that the pasta has a ridged surface, like the penne in this picture.

**Tagliatelle**

**Penne**

**Tortellini**

Filled pasta usually contains meat, cheese, fish or vegetables.

**Tortelloni**

**Farfalle**

**Fusilli**

**Macaroni**

**Ravioli**

**Conchiglie**

# Spaghetti bolognese

This well-known pasta dish comes from the city of Bologna in Northern Italy. It is spaghetti served with a meat sauce. Don't overcook the spaghetti. It should be "al dente" - soft on the outside but still firm inside.

1 medium onion
1 medium carrot
1 stick of celery
7 rashers rindless streaky bacon
1 clove of garlic
2 tablespoons olive oil
450g/1lb. minced beef
400g/14oz. can tomatoes
2 tablespoons tomato purée
pinch of dried oregano or mixed herbs
salt and black pepper
340g/12oz. dried spaghetti

Sprinkle some finely-grated Parmesan cheese onto the sauce before you serve it.

1. Peel and chop the onion, carrot and celery finely. Cut the bacon into narrow strips. Peel and crush the garlic.

2. Heat the oil in a large saucepan. Cook the onion, carrot, celery and garlic over a low heat until they are soft.

3. Add the minced beef and chopped bacon. Cook them until the meat has browned, stirring all the time.

4. Stir in the canned tomatoes, tomato purée and oregano. Taste the sauce and season it with a little salt and pepper.

5. Put the lid on the pan and let the sauce simmer for 30 minutes. Stir it occasionally to stop it from sticking.

6. Meanwhile, start to cook the spaghetti. Heat some water in a large saucepan. Add a pinch of salt.

7. When the water boils, gently push the spaghetti down into the pan until it is covered with water.

8. Boil the spaghetti for 12-15 minutes. Drain it in a colander over a sink. Serve straightaway with the sauce.

# Pizza

Pizzas are now known all over the world, but they originally came from southern Italy. This recipe is for a basic pizza, topped with tomato sauce and cheese. There are also suggestions of toppings you could add. Allow at least 1½ hours to make this pizza, as you have to leave time for the dough to rise. This recipe makes a 25cm (10in.) pizza, enough for two.

175g/6oz. strong white bread flour
½ teaspoon salt
½ teaspoon caster sugar
1 teaspoon easy-blend dried yeast
1 dessertspoon olive oil
125ml/4 fl oz. hot water
200g/7oz. can tomatoes, drained
1 dessertspoon tomato purée
1 teaspoon sugar
salt and pepper
55g/2oz. cheese

Oven temperature:
230°C/450°F/Gas mark 8

1. Sift the flour, salt, sugar and yeast into a bowl. Mix them together, then add the olive oil and water.

**You can try adding different toppings to your pizza. Here are some suggestions:**

**Tuna and sweetcorn**

**Red pepper, sliced black olives and anchovies**

**Mozzarella cheese and pepperoni**

2. Mix everything to make a ball of dough, using a wooden spoon first, then squeeze it with your hands.

3. Sprinkle flour onto a work surface. Put the dough onto it and knead it for five minutes, until it is smooth and stretchy.

4. Grease a bowl and put the dough into it. Cover the bowl with a cloth and put it in a warm place for an hour.

5. Turn on the oven. When the dough has doubled in size, knead it again for a few minutes more.

6. Put the dough on a greased baking tray and press it into a circle about 25cm (10in.) across and 1cm (½ in.) thick.

7. Cook the tomatoes, tomato purée, sugar, salt and pepper together in a frying pan for 10 minutes.

8. Spread the tomato sauce over the pizza base. Sprinkle it with grated cheese and add any topping you like.

9. Bake the pizza on the top shelf of the oven for 12-15 minutes, until the edges are golden and the cheese is bubbling.

# Italian delicatessens

You will probably find an Italian delicatessen in most large cities around the world. Their shelves and counters are usually stocked with a huge range of traditional Italian food and ingredients, such as pasta, cheese, salami, hams and sausages, as well as cans of olives and vegetables preserved in olive oil.

**Many Italian delicatessens, like this one in Bologna in Northern Italy, hang salami and Parma hams from their ceilings.**

# Mediterranean ingredients

The countries around the Mediterranean Sea have a warm, sunny climate with mild winters, so all kinds of vegetables and herbs grow well there. You will find them piled high on market stalls from Spain right across to Greece and the Middle East.

**Tomatoes -** these form one of the main ingredients of Mediterranean cooking. They come in many sizes and are used to make salads and sauces.

**Capers -** these berries are used to add a sharp flavour to many dishes, such as fish, pizzas and sauces.

**Courgette (zucchini) -** this is a baby marrow. It is usually sliced then steamed or fried.

**Sweet peppers -** they have a mild flavour and can be eaten raw or cooked. They can be red, green, yellow or orange.

**Aubergine -** sometimes known as an "eggplant". It is usually sliced and fried, or grilled until soft.

**Artichokes -** usually boiled, the flesh from the leaves and the soft heart are eaten.

# Herbs

Herbs, such as rosemary, thyme, oregano, bay and basil, grow in Mediterranean countries. They are an important ingredient, especially in meat and fish recipes.

**Rosemary**

**Bay leaves -** used fresh or dried, bay leaves add flavour to sauces.

**Thyme**

**Oregano**

**Rosemary, thyme and oregano -** these herbs are used fresh or dried. They are chopped finely and added to many dishes.

**Basil -** goes very well with tomatoes. French and Italian cooks rip the leaves into pieces and use them in sauces, soups and sprinkled over salads.

**Onions -** there are several kinds of onions. They are usually cooked and used to add flavour to food. Red onions are sweeter and milder than other onions.

**Lemons -** both the fruit and juice are used widely in Mediterranean cooking. They are squeezed, sliced and sometimes used halved.

**Olive oil**

## Internet link

Go to **www.usborne-quicklinks.com** and enter the keywords "world cookbook" for a link to a website where you can see descriptions of different types of olives.

# Olive oil

Pressed from the pulp of olives, olive oil is used for cooking and to make salad dressings. You can taste its rich flavour in many Mediterranean dishes.

**Olives -** these are the fruit of the olive tree. Black olives are the same as green olives but riper and more juicy.

# England

English cookery includes famous dishes, such as fish and chips, roast beef and Yorkshire pudding, as well as traditional cakes and puddings.

## Scones

Scones are usually served with cream and jam. A meal served with scones and tea is called a cream tea and is very popular in the West of England. This recipe makes about 12 scones.

225g/8oz. self-raising flour
a pinch of salt
55g/2oz. butter
55g/2oz. caster sugar
150ml/5floz. milk

Oven temperature: 220°C/425°F/Gas mark 7

Cut the scones in half and spread them with jam and cream.

### Internet link

Go to **www.usborne-quicklinks.com** and enter the keywords "world cookbook" for a link to a website where you can find out about everyday English foods, such as fish and chips.

This village in the Cotswolds and the surrounding countryside is typical of many parts of England.

1. Turn on the oven. Sift the flour into a large mixing bowl to get rid of any lumps in the flour. Add the salt.

2. Cut the butter into cubes. Rub it into the flour with your fingers until the mixture looks like fine breadcrumbs.

3. Stir in the sugar. Then, add the milk a little at a time, stirring it into the flour mixture with a knife.

4. Flour your hands and gently knead the mixture into a ball. Add one more teaspoon of milk if the mixture seems dry.

5. Sprinkle flour onto your work surface and onto a rolling pin. Roll out the dough until it is about 2cm (¾in.) thick.

6. Use a round cookie cutter or a cup to cut circles out of the mixture. Squeeze the trimmings and roll them again.

7. Cut out as many circles as you can from the dough, then put them on a greased baking sheet.

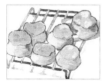

8. Bake the scones near the top of the oven for 12-15 minutes, until golden brown. Let them cool on a rack.

**A traditional afternoon tea in England has small sandwiches, scones, buns and cakes, served with a pot of tea.**

# Afternoon tea

Traditional afternoon tea is usually served in the middle of the afternoon. In the winter, tea is often served by a fire, with hot buttered toast, crumpets, muffins, teabread and fruit cakes.

# Ireland

Ireland is a beautiful country with green hills, many lakes and a spectacular coastline. Potatoes were once the main food in Ireland, so many traditional dishes, such as Irish stew, have potatoes as one of their ingredients. There are potato cakes, potato pancakes and even bread made with potatoes.

## Internet link

Go to **www.usborne-quicklinks.com** and enter the keywords "world cookbook" for a link to a website where you can read more about traditional Irish food and drink.

## Irish stew

This lamb casserole is topped with sliced potatoes. You cook it for a long time, at a low temperature, to make the meat tender. You will need a casserole dish with a lid.

| | |
|---|---|
| 675g/1½ lbs. stewing lamb, or neck and shoulder joints | salt and black pepper |
| | 1 meat stock cube |
| 675g/1½ lbs. medium potatoes | 450ml/¾ pint boiling water |
| 2 large onions | 30g/1oz. butter |
| dried thyme or mixed herbs | Oven temperature: 170°C/325°F/Gas mark 3 |

**This is a typical scene of farmland around Dingle, on the west coast of Ireland.**

1. Use a sharp knife to trim any fat off the lamb. Be careful. Cut the meat into cubes about 2cm/1in. thick.

2. Turn on the oven. Peel the potatoes, then cut them into thin slices. Peel the onions and cut them into small pieces.

3. Put a layer of meat into a casserole dish. Sprinkle it with a little thyme, salt and pepper. Add a layer of onions.

4. Add a layer of potato, then more layers of meat, onions and potato. Sprinkle each layer with thyme, salt and pepper.

5. Make up the stock (see page 4) and pour it into the dish. Melt the butter in a pan. Brush the butter over the top layer of potatoes.

6. Put the lid on the dish and put it in the oven. Cook the stew for two hours. Remove the lid for the last 30 minutes.

When the stew is cooked, the potatoes turn brown and are crisp at the edges.

# Holland

Holland is also known as The Netherlands, which means the low lands. Most of the country is flat, especially the polders, which are areas of land reclaimed from the sea. The landscape is also criss-crossed by canals and dotted with windmills. Dutch food is famous above all for its cheeses, especially Edam and Gouda.

Tiny puffy pancakes, called poffertjes, are sold in many street markets in Holland. They are usually served warm and sprinkled with icing sugar.

## Internet links

Go to **www.usborne-quicklinks.com** and enter the keywords "world cookbook" for links to the following websites:

**Website 1** Find out more about Dutch food and eating habits.

**Website 2** Try a Dutch cheese quiz.

## Cauliflower in cheese sauce

You can make this recipe with any strong-flavoured cheese, such as Cheddar cheese, but to give it a really Dutch flavour, use Edam or Gouda. This is a good dish if you are vegetarian.

115g/4oz. cheese
1 large cauliflower
30g/1oz. butter
30g/1oz. plain flour

300ml/½ pint milk
a pinch of salt and of
    black pepper
a pinch of grated
    nutmeg

Windmills, like these at Stompwijk, are found beside lots of canals in Holland. Windmills were used to pump water into the canals to stop the land from flooding.

1. Grate the cheese. Take the leaves off the cauliflower, then cut out the core. Cut the rest into four pieces.

2. Melt the butter in a pan over a low heat. Add the flour and stir it with a wooden spoon to make a smooth paste.

3. Cook the mixture gently for a minute, then take the pan off the heat. Stir in the milk, a little at a time.

4. Put the pan back on the heat. Let it cook over a low heat for 5-10 minutes, stirring from time to time.

5. Meanwhile, heat a large pan of salted water. When it boils, cook the cauliflower for 5-6 minutes, until tender.

6. Tip the cauliflower into a colander and stand it in a sink to drain. Put the cauliflower into an ovenproof dish.

7. Stir most of the grated cheese into the sauce to melt. Season it with a pinch of salt, pepper and grated nutmeg.

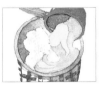

8. When the cheese has melted, pour the sauce over the cauliflower and sprinkle the rest of the cheese on top.

9. Turn on the grill. Put the dish under the grill for a few minutes, until the top starts to bubble and turns brown.

Serve the cauliflower cheese while hot. Be careful as you lift the dish out from under the grill.

# Germany

Germany's landscape ranges from the flat North Sea coast to spectacular river valleys, forests, hills and mountains in the south. German food varies from one end of the country to the other, but it is mostly warming and homely. German specialities are sausages of lots of different kinds, "spätzle" (noodles), thick soups, dumplings and dark rye bread.

### Internet link

Go to www.usborne-quicklinks.com and enter the keywords "world cookbook" for a link to a website where you can discover Germany on an interactive map.

To make Christmas decorations, thread narrow ribbons or gift tape through the holes in the biscuits.

## Lebkuchen

Lebkuchen are spicy German biscuits that are baked around Christmas time. Traditionally they are heart-shaped, but you can get other shapes. The biscuits are decorated with different colours of icing and are hung on Christmas trees. This recipe will make about 15 small biscuits. Double all the quantities if you want to make more.

1 egg
4 tablespoons clear honey
55g/2oz. butter or margarine
55g/2oz. soft brown sugar
225g/8oz. plain flour
1 teaspoon baking powder
2 teaspoons ground ginger

25g/1oz. cocoa powder
1 teaspoon mixed spice
85g/3oz. icing sugar
1 tablespoon lemon juice
food colouring (optional)
icing bag or a cone of greaseproof paper

Oven temperature:
200°C/400°F/Gas mark 6

1. Grease a baking sheet with butter. Separate the egg. Put the yolk into a bowl. You don't need the egg white.

2. Turn on the oven. Put the honey, butter and sugar in a pan over a low heat. Stir them until the butter has melted.

3. Sift the flour, baking powder, cocoa powder, ginger and mixed spice into a mixing bowl. Add the egg yolk.

4. Mix the melted butter, honey and sugar into the flour. Squeeze the mixture into a ball of dough with your hands.

48

In December, many towns in Germany have an outdoor market selling Christmas decorations and food. They are known as "Weihnachtsmarkt" or "Christkindlmarkt".

5. Sprinkle some flour onto a clean worktop and onto a rolling pin. Roll out the dough until it is ½ cm (¼ in.) thick.

6. Use cookie cutters or a knife to cut out different shapes. Roll out the leftover dough and cut out more shapes.

7. Use a spatula to lift the biscuits onto the baking sheet. Make a hole at the top of each biscuit with a skewer.

8. Bake the biscuits for seven to eight minutes, until golden. Then, lift them onto a wire rack and leave them to cool.

9. Meanwhile, sift the icing sugar into a bowl. Mix in the tablespoon of lemon juice, stirring really well.

10. Spoon some of the icing into a smaller bowl. Mix in a few drops of food colouring, if you like.

11. When the biscuits have cooled, spoon the icing into an icing bag. Pipe on the icing slowly by squeezing the bag.

# Austria

Austria is a small country in central Europe. It is completely surrounded by other countries, so has no coastline. It has spectacular scenery, with wooded hills and lakes which are surrounded by high mountains.

Austria is famous for its strudels. These are layers of wafer-thin pastry filled with different kinds of fruit, poppyseeds, or meat. Other specialities are dumplings, bread, noodles, smoked ham and Wiener schnitzel - slices of veal, fried in breadcrumbs.

Let the icing set before you cut the cake.
Serve it with freshly whipped cream.

## Sachertorte

This famous chocolate cake is very rich. Known as 'Sacher's cake', it was first made by a cook called Franz Sacher, who baked it for an Austrian prince.

6 eggs
145g/5oz. softened butter
145g/5oz. caster sugar
225g/8oz. plain chocolate
115g/4oz. plain flour

For the icing:
2 tablespoons butter
225g/8oz. icing sugar
145g/5oz. apricot jam
30g/1oz. cocoa powder

Two 20cm (8in.) sandwich cake tins, greased and lined with a circle of greaseproof paper

Oven temperature:
170°C/325°F/Gas mark 3

1. Separate the eggs. Put the whites in one bowl and the yolks in another. Beat the yolks until smooth.

2. Beat the butter and sugar together with a wooden spoon until creamy. Stir in the egg yolks gradually.

3. Break half the chocolate into pieces in a small heat-proof bowl. Heat a saucepan of water over a low heat.

4. Stand the bowl over the pan and stir the chocolate until it has melted. Stir it into the creamy mixture.

5. Put the egg whites into a large bowl. Whisk them until they are firm and form soft peaks when you lift the whisk.

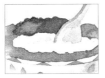

6. Mix the flour into the cake mixture, then fold in the egg whites with a metal spoon. Fold in one spoonful at a time.

7. Pour the mixture into the cake tins. Smooth the top with the back of a spoon. Bake the cakes for 35 minutes.

8. Run a knife around the edge of the cakes to loosen them. Turn them out onto a wire rack and leave them to cool.

9. To make a thick icing. melt the rest of the chocolate in a bowl. Mix in a tablespoon of icing sugar and the butter.

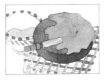

10. Use a knife to spread the chocolate paste onto one half of the cake. Then, put the other cake on top.

11. Melt the jam in a pan over a low heat. Spread it over the top and sides of the cake with a blunt knife.

12. Sift the cocoa powder and the rest of the icing sugar into a bowl. Add water a bit at a time. Spread it all over the cake.

# Coffee houses

Vienna is famous for its coffee houses called Konditoreien. There you can drink different types of coffee, such as Einspänner which has a ball of cream floating in it. They also serve all kinds of delicious cakes, pastries and strudels.

## Internet links

Go to **www.usborne-quicklinks.com** and enter the keywords "world cookbook" for links to the following websites:

**Website 1** Find out more about Austrian food and cooking.

**Website 2** Discover all about Austrian festivities at Christmas.

**In Austria, there are lots of shops, like this one in Vienna, which sell different kinds of cakes and pastries.**

# Switzerland

Switzerland is a small country, right in the centre of Europe, famous for its beautiful mountains and lakes. Swiss people speak four different languages, depending on which part of the country they live in.

## Internet link

Go to **www.usborne-quicklinks.com** and enter the keywords "world cookbook" for a link to a website where you can discover lots of fascinating information and facts about Switzerland.

Muesli is delicious served with fresh fruit, such as strawberries and raspberries.

## Muesli

This healthy breakfast cereal was first invented by a Swiss doctor. It is a tasty mixture of grains, fruit and nuts. You can buy the grains at any health food shop. You will need to start preparing muesli the night before you want to eat it.

1 tablespoon rolled oats
1 tablespoon wheat flakes
1 tablespoon barley flakes
1 tablespoon chopped mixed nuts
6 tablespoons water

1 tablespoon raisins or sultanas
2 tablespoons lemon juice
1 eating apple
milk
1 tablespoon clear honey

1. Before you go to bed, put the oats, wheat flakes and barley flakes into a bowl and pour the water on top.

2. In the morning, peel the apple, cut it in half, then grate it. Put it into a bowl, then stir the lemon juice into it.

3. Gently stir the apple, raisins or sultanas and nuts into the softened oats, wheat flakes and barley flakes.

4. Put the muesli into four bowls and pour on a little milk. Drizzle some honey on top of each helping.

# Raclette

Raclette is traditionally made by melting one side of a block of cheese standing next to an open fire. The melted cheese is scraped off with a knife, and eaten with potatoes, pickled onions and gherkins. In this recipe, the cheese is heated under a grill. Use Swiss Emmental or Gruyère cheese if you can as they taste really good toasted.

4 medium potatoes
a pinch of salt
225g/8oz. cheese

Serve the potatoes while the cheese is still hot.

1. Scrub the potatoes, but do not peel them. Use the tip of a knife to cut out any eyes. Cut the cheese into thin slices.

2. Put the potatoes in a pan of cold, salted water. Bring it to the boil and cook them for 15 to 20 minutes.

3. Check that the potatoes are cooked by pushing a sharp knife into one. It should come out easily.

4. Drain the potatoes and let them cool a little. Cut them in half. Lay the cheese onto the cut side of each potato.

5. Put the potatoes onto a grill rack. Grill them until the cheese melts and starts to bubble.

These cows have been decorated to celebrate their return from the high mountain pastures, where they are taken to graze each summer.

# Cheeses from around the world

There is a huge variety of cheeses around the world. Some are soft and creamy, while others are firmer, with a stronger flavour. Most cheeses are made from cows' milk, but some are made from goats' or sheep's milk. Many cheeses are also used in pastry, sauces, soufflés, pies, pizzas or biscuits.

**Saint André -** a cream cheese from France. It has a soft white rind and a mild flavour.

**Parmesan -** a hard Italian cheese with a strong smell and flavour. It is used grated over pasta or risotto, and in many cooked dishes.

**Emmental**

**Gruyère**

**Camembert -** a cheese from France. It is creamy inside and has a soft rind on the outside.

**Emmental and Gruyère -** firm Swiss cheeses with a slightly sweet, nutty flavour.

**Taleggio -** a creamy, medium-soft Italian cheese with a mild flavour.

**Edam**

**Halloumi -** a mild cheese from Cyprus, made from cows', sheep's or goats' milk.

**Gorgonzola -** a creamy Italian blue cheese with a very strong flavour.

**Gouda and Edam -** mild, buttery Dutch cheeses with a thin rind and wax coating.

**Gouda**

**Goats' cheese -** can be mild and creamy, or firm with a strong taste. Some have a rind.

**Cheddar -** a British cheese with a full, rich flavour. It is often grated and used in cooked dishes.

**Stilton -** a creamy blue-veined English cheese made from cows' milk.

**Smoked cheese -** a mild German cheese with a smoky taste.

**Feta -** a crumbly Greek cheese with a strong, sharp flavour. It is used in salads with tomatoes and olives.

**Manchego -** a firm Spanish cheese with a strong flavour, made from sheep's milk.

**Ricotta -** a mild, low-fat Italian cheese often used for stuffing pasta, such as ravioli.

**Roquefort -** a blue-veined French cheese made from sheep's milk. It has a strong taste.

**Cream cheese -** smooth, buttery cheese often used as a spread or in cheesecakes.

**Mozzarella -** a soft Italian cheese with a mild flavour. It is often used as part of a pizza topping.

## Internet link

Go to **www.usborne-quicklinks.com** and enter the keywords "world cookbook" for a link to a website where you can browse an alphabetical cheese guide with photos and recipe suggestions.

# Hungary

Hungary is a country rich in folklore and traditions, right in the centre of Europe. Its climate is cold in the winter and hot in the summer. Many Hungarian dishes are flavoured with paprika, a spicy powder made from dried red peppers. Onions, tomatoes and sour cream are also used in lots of recipes. Goulash is Hungary's most famous dish, but it is also known for its stuffed cabbage, fish soups, and cottage cheese noodles.

## Internet links

Go to **www.usborne-quicklinks.com** and enter the keywords "world cookbook" for links to the following websites:

**Website 1** Find out more about paprika, a key ingredient used in Hungarian cooking.

**Website 2** Learn about Hungarian food and try some recipes.

Paprika peppers are much smaller than sweet peppers (see page 40). There are different kinds - some much hotter than others.

In rural areas of Hungary, strings of red paprika peppers and garlic are often seen hanging from houses.

## Goulash

This warming stew is flavoured with sweet, spicy paprika and served with dumplings. You need to allow about two hours for it to cook. This lets the meat become really tender. To cook the goulash, you will need a large pan with a lid.

1 large onion
1 clove garlic
4 medium potatoes
2 tablespoons vegetable oil
675g/1½ lb. stewing beef, cut into cubes
400g/14oz. can chopped tomatoes
2 tablespoons paprika
150ml/¼ pint water

half a teaspoon of salt
a pinch of black pepper

For the dumplings:
115g/4oz. plain flour
1 dessertspoon baking powder
big pinch of salt
30g/1oz. butter
1 egg
about 1 tablespoon milk

1. Peel the onion and chop it finely. Peel and crush the garlic. Peel the potatoes and cut them into cubes.

2. Heat the oil in the large pan. Cook the onion and garlic over a low heat until soft. Remove with a spoon.

3. Heat the rest of the oil. When it is hot, add the cubed meat and potatoes and stir them until the meat is brown.

4. Add the onions and the tomatoes, paprika, water, salt and pepper. Stir everything well and turn the heat to low.

5. Put the lid on the pan and cook the goulash over a low heat for about two hours, until the meat is tender.

6. Meanwhile, make the dumplings. Sift the flour into a mixing bowl. Add the baking powder and salt and mix them in.

7. Rub the butter into the flour. Break the egg and stir it in. Add enough milk to make a dough. Squeeze it together.

8. Roll the dough into small balls. Twenty minutes before serving, drop them into the pan. Leave them to cook.

**Serve the goulash with buttered noodles or rice. Sprinkle on a little extra paprika before you serve it.**

# Norway

Norway is part of Scandinavia, a group of the most northern countries in Europe. It is a long, narrow country that stretches for over 2,400 km (1,500 miles) from north to south. The scenery is dramatic, with snow-capped mountains, deep sea inlets called fjords, and huge forests where many different animals live. The winters are long and very cold in Norway, so the Norwegians preserve plenty of food to last them until spring. Meat and fish are often dried, smoked, or preserved with salt.

## Internet link

Go to **www.usborne-quicklinks.com** and enter the keywords "world cookbook" for a link to a website where you can find out more about the culture and history of Norway.

## Red fruit pudding

Many types of berries grow in the Norwegian forests. People make special fruit puddings, like this one, to celebrate the short Scandinavian summer.

450g/1lb. raspberries, blackcurrants or redcurrants, or a mixture of all three
2 tablespoons caster sugar
450ml/¾ pint cold water
2 tablespoons cornflour

1. Put the fruit, sugar and water in a pan. Cook them over a low heat for five minutes, until the fruit is soft.

2. Let the fruit cool, then use the back of a spoon to push it through a sieve into a bowl. Throw away any bits left in the sieve.

In the far North of Norway the sun sets in winter and for 51 days, it is always dark. Reindeer live in the snowy forests.

3. Put the cornflour in a cup. Mix it with a tablespoon of the juices from the cooked fruit, until it is smooth.

4. Stir the cornflour mixture into the fruit. Then, pour the fruit back into the pan and bring it to the boil.

5. Turn the heat down low. Cook the fruit for five minutes, stirring it with a wooden spoon all the time.

6. Take the pan off the heat and let the mixture cool. Pour it into some glasses or bowls. Chill them in a refrigerator.

# Berries

Most berries, such as strawberries, are ripe for picking in the summer. The exceptions are blackberries, which appear early in the autumn, and cranberries, which are ripe in the winter. You can make the Norwegian fruit pudding with any mixture of these berries, but you may need to add more or less sugar to them.

Decorate the puddings with some fresh berries before you serve them.

Strawberries

Blackberries

Blueberries

Redcurrants

Raspberries

Blackcurrants

# Sweden

Like Norway, Denmark and Finland, Sweden forms part of Scandinavia. Half of the country is covered by forests, which are home to reindeer, elk, bears and lynx. Sweden also has a huge number of lakes. The winters are cold and the summers warm in Sweden. It is often known as "The Land of the Midnight Sun" because the sun shines all day and night in the middle of the summer. Swedish food specialities are similar to those in other Scandinavian countries. They include meatballs, liver pâté and smoked meats, as well as smörgåsbord (see pages 62-63). Fish is also popular, especially herring, eel and salmon,

When the dish is cooked, the top layer of potatoes goes crisp golden brown.

## Internet link

Go to **www.usborne-quicklinks.com** and enter the keywords "world cookbook" for a link to a website where you can find out about different festivals which are celebrated throughout Sweden.

## Jansson's temptation

This is a traditional Swedish dish of potatoes and anchovies. There are many stories about how it got its name. Some people think it was named after an opera singer, called Pelle Janzon, while others think it got its name from a film, "The temptation of Jansson".

450g/1lb. potatoes
2 large onions
85g/3oz. butter
2 cans anchovies
a pinch of salt and of pepper
300ml/½ pint double cream or milk

Oven temperature:
200°C/400°F/Gas mark 6

Fresh parsley and dill are used to flavour and decorate many Swedish dishes.

There are over 50,000 islands of different sizes along the coastline of Sweden. Some, like these in the Skaggerak on the west of Sweden, are tiny.

1. Peel the potatoes and cut them into thin strips about 4cm (2in.) long. Put them in a bowl of cold water.

2. Peel the onions and chop them finely. Fry them gently in 30g (1oz.) of the butter until they are soft.

3. Drain the potatoes in a colander. Put a layer of potatoes into a small, heatproof dish. Then, drain the anchovies.

4. Cover the potatoes with a layer of anchovies. Then, cover the anchovies with a layer of the softened onions.

5. Repeat the layers of potato, anchovies and onion to the top of the dish, finishing with a layer of potato.

6. Add the salt and pepper. Then, carefully pour the cream all over the top. It will sink to the bottom of the dish.

7. Cut the rest of the butter into small pieces and dot them around the dish. Bake it for about 45 minutes.

# Denmark

Denmark lies further south than the other countries in Scandinavia, and is separated from them by the sea. The country is actually made up of a peninsular and more than 400 smaller islands. The climate is warm in summer and mild and wet in winter. Denmark has rich farmlands. It is particularly famous for bacon, pork and a wide variety of cheeses.

**Prawns and lemon -** put a lettuce leaf onto the bread. Spoon prawns on top and add some black pepper and a twist of lemon.

## Internet link

Go to **www.usborne-quicklinks.com** and enter the keywords "world cookbook" for a link to a website where you can discover more delicious ideas for smørrebrød and other Danish recipes.

## Smørrebrød

Smørrebrød are open sandwiches. The sandwiches can be made with any ingredients and are usually eaten with a knife and fork. The best bread to use is dark rye bread. To make the sandwiches, butter the bread then lay the ingredients on top.

**Salami and tomato -** cover the bread with slices of salami. Add slices of tomato and some onion rings.

## Preparing ingredients

Cut the stalk off the lettuce, then tear off as many leaves as you need. Wash and dry the leaves on kitchen paper.

Peel an onion and cut off the ends. Slice the onion finely, then separate the slices to make onion rings.

## Hard-boiling eggs

1. To hard-boil eggs, heat some water in a pan until it bubbles. Then, boil the eggs for ten minutes.

2. Put the eggs into a bowl of cold water. Tap each egg on the edge of the bowl to crack the shell, then peel it off.

**Blue cheese and lettuce -** cover the bread with lettuce and thin slices of blue cheese. Sprinkle cress on top.

# Fish

Salmon and herring are used in lots of Danish dishes and are prepared in many different ways. For example, gravlax is raw salmon which has been soaked in a mixture of salt, sugar and dill.

Tall buildings, like these, line the edge of many fishing harbours in Denmark.

**Smoked salmon and egg -** cover the bread with slices of hard-boiled egg and smoked salmon. Sprinkle it with chopped dill.

**Cheese and tomato -** lay thin slices of cheese on the bread. Then, lay a row of sliced tomato along the middle. Add a gherkin garnish.

# Garnishes

**Cress and herring -** lay slices of hard-boiled egg and fillet of pickled herring on the bread. Sprinkle it with cress.

Cut a slice of lemon in half. Make a cut in the middle of each half, then twist the ends so that the slice stands up.

Make thin cuts along the length of a gherkin, cutting almost to the end. Then, spread the slices out like a fan.

# Russia

Russia is in Asia. It is the biggest of the countries that used to form the Soviet Union. It is very cold in Russia in the winter, so root vegetables, such as potatoes, beetroot and turnips grow well there. In the summer, wheat and other grains are grown on the Russian steppes, the huge grasslands in the middle of the country. Russian specialities include small pancakes made from buckwheat flour, called blinis, and borscht, a ruby-red soup made from beetroot and soured cream. Because the country is so big and varied, each area has its own cooking traditions.

This is St. Basil's Cathedral. It was built in the 1550s and stands at one end of Red Square in Moscow.

### Internet link

Go to **www.usborne-quicklinks.com** and enter the keywords "world cookbook" for a link to a website where you can read about Russian food and see a menu from a St. Petersburg restaurant.

## Beef stroganoff

The former Russian court was very wealthy. This quick and delicious recipe was first created in the 1700s for Count Alexander Stroganoff. The recipe uses expensive steak, so it is best to cook it on special occasions.

| | |
|---|---|
| 115g/4oz. mushrooms | salt and black pepper |
| 1 medium onion | 55g/2oz. butter |
| 450g/1lb. rump or fillet steak | 1 teaspoon smooth mustard |
| | 150ml/¼ pint soured cream |

1. Wipe the mushrooms clean, then slice them. Cut the ends off the onion and peel it, then cut it into thin slices.

2. Cut the steak into narrow strips about 6cm (2½in.) long. Sprinkle them with a little salt and pepper.

**Serve the stroganoff hot with egg noodles or boiled rice.**

3. Melt the butter in a large frying pan. Fry the onion slices over a low heat until soft, stirring all the time.

4. Add the sliced mushrooms to the pan, stir them in and cook them for two minutes. Stir in the mustard.

5. Add the steak. Cook the mixture for about five minutes, stirring all the time, until the meat is brown on both sides.

6. Turn the heat down and stir in the cream. Cook the stroganoff gently for another two minutes, then serve.

# A Russian delicacy

Caviar is the salted roe, or eggs, of a big fish called a sturgeon. It is usually served as a starter. The best and most expensive caviar in the world comes from Russia.

**You can get different colours of caviar, depending on which fish it comes from. The most expensive caviar is black.**

# Bread from around the world

In parts of the world where wheat and other grains grow, bread has been baked for hundreds of years. A lot of bread is made from wheat flour, but it can also be made from rye, barley, oats or maize (corn). In many countries, people eat flat breads which don't contain anything that make them rise. In other places, they eat bread that has had yeast or something else added to it to make it rise.

These Egyptian bakers are making a type of flat bread.

**Croissants -** flaky crescents of bread layered with butter. They are often eaten in France for breakfast.

**Brioche -** a sweet French bread made as a loaf or as buns.

**Challah -** a rich bread, usually plaited, which is traditionally made for Jewish holy days.

**Pretzels -** German bread shapes, covered in salt. They are also popular in America.

**Bagels -** soft bread rings with a chewy crust. Bagels are a Jewish speciality.

**Sourdough rye bread -** a dense bread popular in Russia and much of Eastern Europe.

**Baguette -** a stick of French bread. It is soft and white inside, and has a crisp crust.

**Barbari -** a Middle Eastern flat bread.

**Hard dough bread -** a Caribbean bread, made with soya flour.

**Pitta bread -** a Middle Eastern flat bread which can be split and filled.

**Farmhouse loaf -** a soft, white British loaf with a thick crust.

**Naan -** an Indian flat bread.

**Dark rye bread -** is eaten in Germany and many Eastern European countries.

**Soda bread -** traditional Irish bread, usually made with brown flour.

**Focaccia -** an Italian bread which is often flavoured with olives, garlic or herbs and sprinkled with crushed salt.

## Internet link

Go to **www.usborne-quicklinks.com** and enter the keywords "world cookbook" for a link to a website where you can find out about how bread is made and read lots of fascinating facts about its history.

# Greece

Greece lies in southern Europe, on the Mediterranean Sea. The climate is warm and sunny. Much of Greece is mountainous and the land is rocky and bare, but olive and lemon trees grow well there and sheep and goats graze the hills. Well-known Greek dishes include avgolemono, an egg and lemon soup, and spanakopita, a type of spinach pie. It is also famous for tzatziki, a yogurt, garlic and cucumber mixture, which is often eaten as a starter with pitta bread.

## Internet link

Go to **www.usborne-quicklinks.com** and enter the keywords "world cookbook" for a link to a website where you can read about the history of Greek cooking, discover the ingredients used in Greek cooking and find some delicious recipes.

## Moussaka

This is a traditional Greek dish made of lamb and aubergine, with a creamy topping. You will need an ovenproof casserole dish.

1 large aubergine
1 large onion
1 clove garlic
4 tablespoons oil
450g/1lb. minced lamb
400g/14oz. can
  tomatoes
1 tablespoon tomato
  purée
1 teaspoon ground
  cinnamon

a pinch of salt and of
  pepper
2 eggs
55g/2oz. butter
2 tablespoons plain flour
600ml/1 pint milk
55g/2oz. Cheddar cheese

Oven temperature:
190ºC/375ºF/Gas mark 5

1. Turn on the oven. Cut the aubergine into thin slices. Peel and chop the onion, and peel and crush the clove of garlic.

2. Heat two tablespoons of the oil in a pan which has a lid. Fry the onions and garlic gently, until they are soft.

3. Add the minced lamb, breaking it up with a spoon. Fry it, stirring well until it is brown all over.

4. Stir in the tomatoes, tomato purée, cinnamon, salt and pepper. Cook gently for 20 minutes with the lid on.

5. Heat the rest of the oil in a frying pan and fry the aubergine slices until they are soft. Add more oil if needed.

6. Spoon half the meat mixture into the bottom of a casserole dish. Cover it with a layer of the sliced aubergine.

Olive trees like these, can be seen growing in the Greek countryside.

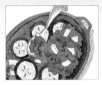

7. Repeat the layers one more time, finishing with a layer of aubergine. Then, break the eggs into a bowl and beat them.

8. Melt the butter in a pan. Stir in the flour to make a smooth paste. Cook it gently for a minute, stirring well.

9. Take the pan off the heat and stir in the milk. Then, heat the sauce until it boils. Let it cool, then stir in the egg.

10. Pour the sauce over the moussaka. Sprinkle it with grated cheese and bake it in the oven for 45 minutes.

When the moussaka is cooked, the topping turns crispy and golden brown. Serve it hot, with a mixture of green salad leaves.

# Turkey

Turkey lies at the eastern end of the Mediterranean Sea. Part of the country is in Europe, but most of it is in Asia, so it has always been influenced by both continents. Turkey was once the centre of a huge empire and has always been known for its fine cooking and traditional dishes. Popular Turkish dishes include rice dishes called pilaffs, stuffed vegetables, milk puddings flavoured with orange blossom or rosewater and delicious sweet, nutty pastries. Grilled or baked fish is also a common dish, especially along the Mediterranean coast.

**You can serve the kebabs with long-grain rice instead of pitta bread, if you prefer.**

## Internet link

Go to **www.usborne-quicklinks.com** and enter the keywords "world cookbook" for a link to a website where you can find out more about Turkish food and its history. There are also Turkish words and phrases, and lots of recipes.

Oregano          Rosemary

Lemon

## Shish kebabs

Shish kebabs are cubes of meat cooked on a skewer. You can use metal or wooden skewers to make them. If you use wooden skewers, soak them in water for 30 minutes first, to stop them from burning. You need to allow an hour for soaking the meat in a sauce first. This makes it more tender.

675g/1½ lbs. lamb
4 tablespoons olive oil
4 tablespoons lemon juice
½ teaspoon dried or fresh chopped oregano
a large pinch of salt and of black pepper
8 lettuce leaves

4 tomatoes
half a cucumber
½ teaspoon dried or fresh rosemary
8 pitta breads

8 metal or wooden skewers

1. Put the lamb on a chopping board and carefully use a sharp knife to cut it into cubes about 2cm (1in.) across.

2. Put the olive oil, three tablespoons of lemon juice, the oregano and salt and pepper into a bowl. Mix them well.

3. Put the meat in the bowl and stir it. Leave the meat to soak in the oil and lemon mixture for an hour.

4. Wash and dry the lettuce, then cut it into strips. Slice the cucumber and cut the tomatoes into quarters.

5. Push six cubes of meat onto each skewer, leaving gaps between them. Sprinkle them with a little rosemary.

6. Heat the grill and cook the kebabs for 10-12 minutes. Turn them every so often so they are brown all over.

7. Turn the grill down and warm the pitta breads under it quickly. Then, slice each one along the top.

8. Fill each pitta bread with some salad and the meat from one kebab. Sprinkle with a little more lemon juice.

# Turkish coffee

Turkey is famous for its coffee which is very strong and sweet. The coffee is freshly roasted and ground when it is needed. Traditionally it is brewed in a brass or copper coffee pot called an ibrik. Coffee cups are small and often have no handles.

If you go to Turkey, you may see elaborate coffee urns, like these from a shop window in Ankara.

# The Middle East

## Tabbouleh

The area called the Middle East is very warm and dry. It stretches from North Africa across to southern Russia. The Middle East includes many different countries, races and religions. Despite their differences, all the countries have similar ways of preparing food.

**Dried dates**

This salad comes from Lebanon, on the eastern side of the Mediterranean Sea. It is made with chopped herbs, fresh vegetables, and a grain, called cracked wheat. All the ingredients are tossed in a delicious dressing, with a lemony taste.

**Date palm trees, like this one, grow throughout the Middle East. The dates grow in huge clusters at the bottom of the large leaves.**

225g/8oz. cracked wheat
55g/2oz. parsley
30g/1oz. fresh mint
3 tomatoes
half a cucumber
6 spring onions

8 lettuce leaves

For the dressing:
6 tablespoons olive oil
2 lemons
salt and black pepper

1. Put the cracked wheat in a bowl and cover it with boiling water. Leave it to soak for about 20 minutes.

2. Chop the parsley, mint, tomatoes and cucumber finely. Trim the ends off the spring onions and slice them.

3. When the wheat is soft, tip it into a sieve. Press it with the back of a spoon to squeeze out any excess water.

4. Wash the lettuce leaves and pat them dry. Cut the lemons in half and squeeze out the juice.

5. To make the dressing, mix the olive oil, six tablespoons of lemon juice, and a pinch of salt and black pepper.

6. Put the wheat into a bowl. Mix in all the other chopped ingredients. Pour on the dressing and mix well.

**If you visit a market in the Middle East you will see bowls, like these, filled with spices.**

**To serve, put two lettuce leaves on each person's plate and spoon some tabbouleh on top.**

## Internet link

Go to **www.usborne-quicklinks.com** and enter the keywords "world cookbook" for a link to a website where you can discover all about different Middle Eastern ingredients and dishes.

# Hummus

Creamy dips are a popular starter or "mezze" in the Middle East, Greece and Turkey. They are made from many different things, such as smoked fish or puréed aubergines. Hummus is a delicious garlicky dip made from chickpeas. It also contains tahina (tahini), a thick oily paste made from sesame seeds. You can buy tahina in large supermarkets or health food stores.

400g/14oz. can of
  chickpeas
1 clove garlic
2 lemons
2 tablespoons olive oil
1 tablespoon light
  tahina paste
3 tablespoons milk

a pinch of salt and
  of black pepper

To serve:
1 tablespoon finely
  chopped parsley
paprika

1. Open the can of chickpeas and drain them into a colander. Shake it gently to get rid of any excess liquid.

2. Put the chickpeas into a blender if you have one, or push them through a sieve with a spoon, to make a paste.

3. Peel the clove of garlic and crush it with a fork or in a garlic press. Cut the lemons in half and squeeze the juice out.

4. Mix six tablespoons of lemon juice, the garlic, oil, tahina, milk, and salt and pepper into the chickpea paste.

**Sprinkle the hummus with chopped parsley and paprika. Serve it with warmed pitta bread and some olives.**

## Chickpeas

Chickpeas, also known as garbanzo beans or ceci beans, are used in many Middle Eastern dishes. They are also used in recipes in some Mediterranean countries and India. Chickpeas grow in pods about 1in. long, with only one or two chickpeas growing in each pod. They are light brown, slightly larger than peas and have a mild nutty taste.

# Halva

Halva is popular in Middle Eastern countries, and in India. It is a sweet served at the end of a meal, often with a cup of strong, sweet coffee or a glass of mint tea. You will need a shallow dish about 25cm (10in.) across.

85g/3oz. caster sugar
300ml/½ pint water
115g/4oz. butter
115g/4oz. semolina
2 drops vanilla extract
   or essence

**Decorate the top of each piece of halva with a flaked almond.**

1. Put the sugar and water in a pan. Cook them over a low heat until the sugar dissolves. Remove from the heat.

2. Melt the butter in another pan. Add the semolina and cook it for three minutes, stirring all the time.

3. Off the heat, add the vanilla, then stir in the syrup made from the sugar and water. Return the pan to the heat.

4. Stir the mixture for three minutes, until it is really thick. Pour it into a dish. Smooth the top, let it set, then cut it into squares.

# Mezze

Mezze are small dishes served at the beginning of a meal, but people in the Middle East also eat them as snacks with drinks at any time. Typical mezze are bowls of nuts, dips, olives, stuffed vine leaves and salads.

**Mezze**

# Cakes and pastries

Many countries have their own traditional cakes, pastries and cookies, especially in Europe, the Middle East, Asia and North America. The recipes are usually based on local ingredients and many are baked for special occasions.

**Macaroons -** small, sweet biscuits made from ground almond and egg whites. The most famous macaroons are Italian amaretti.

## Internet link

Go to **www.usborne-quicklinks.com** and enter the keywords "world cookbook" for a link to a website where you can find out about the legend of Chinese moon cakes.

**Carrot cake -** a sweet American cake made with grated carrots. It is topped with cream cheese icing.

**Pecan pie -** traditionally from the Southern states of America. It has a sweet, crunchy pecan nut filling and is often served with whipped cream.

**American muffins -** sweet, light, small cakes, often flavoured with fruit or chocolate.

**Indian cakes -** these are really sweets rather than cakes. They tend to be very sweet, for example jalebi are deep-fried and soaked in syrup, and barfi are made with condensed milk and nuts.

Jalebi

Barfi

**Profiterôles** - small buns of choux pastry originally from France. They are topped with chocolate and filled with cream. Chocolate éclairs are the same, but are a different shape.

**Panettone** - a spicy Italian fruit bread traditionally eaten at Christmas. It is usually sold in big decorated boxes.

**Fruit tarts -** little tarts with a pastry base, sometimes filled with custard. They are popular in European pâtisseries.

**Panforte** - a rich, dense, spicy cake from Siena in Italy. It is usually cut into small slices and eaten with coffee.

**Baklava** - very sweet cake popular in Greece and the Middle East. It is made of wafer-thin filo pastry filled with nuts and soaked in honey.

**Konafa (kadeifi) -** a syrupy sweet Middle Eastern cake made from pastry that looks a bit like fine spaghetti. You can buy the pastry ready-made in Greek and Turkish shops.

**Chinese cakes -** tend to be very sweet. Moon cakes are traditionally made to celebrate the Harvest moon festival.

**Moon cakes**

Konafa

# India

India is a big country of contrasts, ranging from the Himalayan mountains to hot, dry plains and steamy rainforests. Over 300 million people live there. Each region in India has its own special dishes, often influenced by different religions. Indian food tastes quite different from other food because of the unique mixtures of spices and flavourings that Indian cooks use.

The Taj Mahal at Agra, India

## Internet link

Go to **www.usborne-quicklinks.com** and enter the keywords "world cookbook" for a link to a website where you can search through an extensive glossary of Indian cooking ingredients.

A vegetable stall in a bazaar in Pushkar, Rajasthan. Stalls like this one, sell crops which are grown locally.

## Basmati rice

The best rice for Indian cooking is Basmati rice. To stop the grains from sticking together, soak the rice in cold water for 30 minutes first, then follow the cooking instructions on the packet. When the rice is cooked, fluff it up with a fork.

# Bhuna gosht

This is a spicy lamb dish. For a filling meal, serve it with rice, dhal (lentil stew) and raita (a yoghurt and cucumber dish). The recipes for dhal and raita are on page 80.

1 onion
2 cloves garlic
3 medium tomatoes
675g/1½lbs. lean lamb
a pinch of salt
4 tbs. lemon juice
55g/2oz. butter
1 tsp. chilli powder
2 tsp. ground coriander

1 tsp. ground cumin
1 tsp. turmeric
1 tsp. black pepper
1 meat stock cube
300ml/½ pint boiling
  water
400g/14oz. can
  tomatoes

Put the bhuna gosht into a warm dish and serve it with rice.

1. Peel the onion and chop it. Peel and crush the garlic with a fork or a press. Cut the fresh tomatoes into quarters.

2. Cut the lamb into cubes. Add the salt and the lemon juice. Mix it well, then leave it to soak for 15 minutes.

3. Melt the butter in a frying pan. Cook the onion and garlic over a low heat for about five minutes, until soft.

4. Stir all the spices, the pepper, onion, garlic and tomatoes into the lamb. Then pour everything into a deep pan.

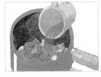

5. Make the stock and add it to the pan. Add the can of tomatoes. Let it bubble over a low heat, stirring occasionally.

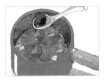

6. Cook the mixture for 20-25 minutes. Stir in a tiny bit more chilli powder if you want it to taste really spicy.

# Dhal

Dhal (dal) is an Indian word for all pulses, such as dried beans, split peas and lentils. Pulses form the main part of many meals in India, because lots of people are vegetarian. This is a recipe for a thick, spicy lentil stew, which is also called dhal.

1 clove garlic
1 small onion
225g/8oz. red lentils
55g/2oz. butter
pinch of chilli powder
1 teaspoon ground cumin
1 teaspoon turmeric
450ml/¾ pint water
pinch of salt

1. Peel and crush the garlic with a fork or in a garlic press. Peel the onion and chop it. Rinse the lentils in a sieve.

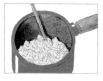

2. Melt the butter in a deep pan. Gently cook the garlic and onion for three to five minutes until they are soft.

3. Add the chilli powder, turmeric, cumin, lentils and water. Bring the mixture to the boil, stirring all the time.

4. Turn the heat down and let the mixture simmer for about 20 minutes until the lentils are soft.

5. Take the pan off the heat and add the salt. Beat the mixture well with a wooden spoon until it's nearly smooth.

# Cucumber raita

Raitas are made of natural yogurt mixed with fresh vegetables, herbs and sometimes nuts. They are served with spicy dishes to provide a contrasting taste and to cool your mouth down.

handful fresh mint leaves
half a cucumber
300ml/½ pint thick
   natural yogurt
pinch of salt and of
   black pepper

1. Wash the mint leaves and shake them dry. Strip the leafy part away from their stalks, then chop the leaves finely.

2. Peel the green skin off the cucumber, then cut it into slices lengthways. Cut the slices into small strips.

3. Whisk the yogurt in a bowl until it is smooth. Stir in the cucumber and mint and season with salt and pepper.

# Contrasting flavours

A typical Indian meal is made up of several dishes with contrasting savoury, sweet and spicy flavours, colours and textures. There is usually a meat dish, a dhal, a vegetable dish, rice, a raita and maybe fresh mango or lime chutney and bread, such as a puri or chapatti. The food is served in small metal bowls called katoris. They are often put on a large tray called a thali, so meals like this are called thalis too.

A thali tray with bowls of basmati rice, raita, bhuna gosht and dhal.

Basmati rice

Cucumber raita

Dhal

Bhuna gosht

# Thailand

Thailand is in south-east Asia and has a tropical climate with sunshine all the year round. It has white beaches fringed with palm trees, lush rainforests, rivers and waterfalls. Thai food is colourful, fresh and spicy. Thai cooks use blends of spices, particularly chillies, lemon grass, coriander and a salty fish paste, called "nam pla".

## Internet link

Go to **www.usborne-quicklinks.com** and enter the keywords "world cookbook" for a link to a website where you can find lots of recipes and pictures of popular dishes from Thailand that you might find on a menu in a Thai restaurant.

## Chicken in coconut sauce

Coconut adds a creamy taste to this typical Thai dish. You can also taste the blend of garlic, chilli powder and ground ginger.

| | |
|---|---|
| 2 medium onions | 3 tablespoons vegetable oil |
| 3 cloves garlic | 4 skinless chicken breasts |
| 1 teaspoon ground ginger | 1 lemon |
| 1 teaspoon chilli powder | 55g/2oz. creamed coconut |
| a pinch of salt and of black pepper | 300ml/½ pint hot water |

**In parts of Thailand, there are floating markets, where you can buy fruit, vegetables and cooked food from people in boats.**

Serve the chicken with boiled or spiced rice. You could sprinkle freshly-chopped coriander leaves on top.

1. Peel and chop the onions, and peel and crush the garlic. Mix the ginger, chilli powder, salt and pepper in a bowl.

2. Heat the oil in a large frying pan. Add the chicken breasts and cook them gently for five minutes on each side.

3. Lift the chicken breasts onto a paper towel. Pat them with another paper towel to remove any extra oil.

4. Cut the lemon in half and squeeze it. Sprinkle the chicken with the spice mixture and some lemon juice.

5. Grate the creamed coconut finely. Put it in a bowl with the hot water and whisk it until it looks like milk.

6. Heat the oil in the frying pan again. Cook the onions and garlic over a low heat until they are soft.

7. Put the chicken back in the frying pan and pour the coconut mixture over it. Stir everything together.

8. Cook the chicken for about 20 minutes, until it is cooked right through. Get someone to check this for you.

# Spices

The rich flavours of Indian, Thai and Indonesian food come from the many different spices cooks use. A dish can contain just one spice or as many as fifteen. The mixtures of freshly-ground spices and herbs used in Indian cooking are called masalas and each one has its own distinctive flavour. Curry powder is a ready-made masala. Spices are not always "hot". Hot foods are usually flavoured with chillies. Other spices come from dried roots, bark, seeds, berries and other fruit.

**Turmeric -** this spice colours food yellow and has a strong, slightly bitter flavour.

**Mustard seeds -** when cooked in oil, these seeds give food a delicious nutty flavour.

**Cumin seeds -** these have an earthy flavour and are used a lot in Indian cooking.

**Coriander seeds -** these are usually ground and have a delicate flavour.

**Lemon grass -** lemony-flavoured stems used to flavour dishes, such as rice.

**Fresh ginger -** a knobbly brown "root". It is peeled, then grated.

**Kaffir lime leaves -** these have a spicy lime flavour and are added to many Thai and Indonesian dishes. They are removed at the end of cooking.

**Many spices are dried before they are used. This shows cloves being laid out to dry in the sun in North Moluccas, Indonesia.**

**Nutmeg -** this spice is grated into a powder. It is used to add flavour to savoury dishes in Asia.

**Grated nutmeg**

**Whole cloves -** used in rice and meat dishes, they have a strong flavour.

**Chilli powder and red chillies -** these give food a hot, fiery flavour.

**Garlic -** each head of garlic is made up of individual cloves.

**Cardamom pods -** these sweetly-flavoured dried seed pods are used either whole or ground in both sweet and savoury dishes. Sometimes just the seeds are used.

In spice markets, like this one in Istanbul in Turkey, spices are sold loose by weight.

**Cinnamon sticks**

**Cinnamon -** the dried inner bark of a tropical tree. The sticks are used whole in meat and rice dishes, and are not eaten. Ground cinnamon is often used to flavour cakes and biscuits.

## Internet links

Go to **www.usborne-quicklinks.com** and enter the keywords "world cookbook" for links to the following websites:

**Website 1** Search for a specific spice and find out interesting facts and tips on using spices.

**Website 2** Read a history of the spice trade and find out who controlled the spice routes.

# Preparing spices

Indian, Thai and Indonesian cooks usually buy spices whole and grind them into a powder when they need them. This way, the spices stay fresh and keep their flavour for longer. Before grinding some spices, such as cumin and coriander, cooks dry-roast them.

1. To roast a spice, heat a frying pan over a medium heat. Add the spices and cook them for about two minutes.

2. Shake the pan so that the spices are roasted evenly. This also stops them from sticking. Take them off the heat when they turn darker.

To grind whole spices, put them into a deep bowl, called a mortar. Use the pestle to crush them into a fine powder.

# China

Chinese cooking is famous around the world for its mixture of dishes and flavours. China is a vast country and the dishes vary greatly from one region to another. In the south, dishes include lots of fish and seafood, whereas meat, particularly pork, is eaten more often in the north. In the central regions the food is spicy and contains garlic and chillies. In most Chinese meals, the main dish is usually rice or noodles, accompanied by a variety of savoury dishes.

Rice is one of China's main crops. It is grown in huge paddy fields which are flooded with water.

## Fried rice with vegetables

Lots of Chinese cooking is stir-fried. All the ingredients have to be cut up into small pieces about the same size, then cooked quickly over a high heat.

15g/½oz. butter
225g/8oz. long grain rice
450ml/¾ pint water
½ teaspoon salt
6 mushrooms
¼ small head of Chinese leaves
6 spring onions

1 clove garlic
2cm/1in. cube fresh root ginger
2 tablespoons sunflower oil
115g/4oz. frozen peas
145g/5oz. bean sprouts
1-2 tablespoons soy sauce

1. Melt the butter in a pan over a low heat. Stir in the rice and cook it for a few minutes until it becomes transparent.

2. Add the water and salt, then put a lid on the pan. Cook the rice gently for 15 minutes without stirring it.

3. The rice is cooked when it is tender and has absorbed all the water. Bite a few grains to check they are done.

4. Wipe the mushrooms and slice them. Slice the Chinese leaves into strips. Cut the spring onions into 2cm/1in. slices.

5. Peel and crush the clove of garlic. Peel the ginger and grate it using the large holes of a cheese grater.

6. Heat the sunflower oil in a frying pan until hot. Fry the garlic and ginger for 30 seconds, stirring all the time.

7. Add the mushrooms and cook them over a high heat for another two minutes, still stirring. Stir in the spring onions.

8. Add the peas, rice, Chinese leaves and bean sprouts. Stir everything over a high heat for about five minutes.

9. When the vegetables are just tender, sprinkle the soy sauce over them and stir-fry them for another two minutes.

## Internet link

Go to **www.usborne-quicklinks.com** and enter the keywords "world cookbook" for a link to a website where you can take a virtual journey of China and discover the history of Chinese food, regional specialities and recipes.

Spoon the stir-fried rice into a warm serving dish and serve while still hot.

# Sweet and sour spare ribs

Chinese dishes often combine flavours that are quite different from each other. You will need to start preparing this recipe about one hour and 20 minutes before eating it, as the meat has to soak in a sauce for an hour.

675g/1½ lbs. pork spare ribs
½ tsp. salt
2 tbsp. caster sugar
1 tbsp. light soy sauce
2 tbsp. wine vinegar

1½ tbsp. tomato purée
2 tbsp. orange juice
1 small onion
2cm/1in. cube fresh ginger
1 clove garlic
3 tbsp. vegetable oil

1. Rinse the spare ribs and pat them dry with a paper towel. Cut off as much of the fat as you can. Sprinkle with salt.

2. Pour the sugar, soy sauce, vinegar, tomato purée and orange juice into a deep casserole dish and stir them well.

**Lift the spare ribs onto a warm serving plate and pour the sauce in the pan over them. Serve them with boiled rice.**

3. Put the ribs into the sauce and cover them with plastic foodwrap. Leave them to soak in the sauce for an hour.

4. Peel the onion and chop it finely. Peel the ginger and grate it. Peel and crush the garlic with a fork or in a press.

5. Heat the oil in a large frying pan. Fry the onion, ginger and garlic for a few minutes, then remove them from the pan.

6. Then, fry the ribs over a high heat for about five minutes, turning them over half way through.

7. Turn the heat down a little. Add the onion, garlic and ginger. Pour the sauce from the casserole dish over the top.

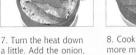
8. Cook for about 10 more minutes until the ribs are cooked, stirring them all the time so they do not burn.

# Using chopsticks

Chinese food is usually eaten with chopsticks, made from wood, bamboo or plastic. If you want to try eating with chopsticks, you'll need to practise holding them. It can be quite tricky at first.

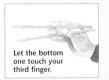
**Let the bottom one touch your third finger.**

**The bottom one should stay still.**

1. Hold the top chopstick between your first two fingers. Rest the bottom one in the 'v' between your finger and thumb.

2. Move your first finger to make the top chopstick move up and down. The ends will pinch together to pick up food.

# Soy sauce

Soy sauce is a salty sauce used to add flavour, and sometimes colour, to Chinese cooking. It is made from soya beans, wheat flour, water and salt. Soy sauce is added to cooked dishes, such as stir-fries, and is often used in a marinade, a sauce which meat is soaked in, to make it more tender.

# Japan

Grains of rice grow at the top of long stalks. The stalks are dried, then the rice grains are removed by machines.

Japan is made up of four main islands to the east of China. The Japanese eat a lot of fish, seafood, vegetables, noodles and rice. Japanese food is very light and low in fat. It is often served raw or only lightly cooked and is some of the healthiest food in the world.

## Internet links

Go to **www.usborne-quicklinks.com** and enter the keywords "world cookbook" for links to the following websites:

**Website 1** Find out the meaning of the Japanese word "gohan".

**Website 2** Search through an excellent glossary of Japanese dishes, spices and ingredients.

## Vegetable casserole

This is a traditional winter dish in Japan, cooked in a casserole dish with a lid. It is usually served with rice or noodles and a tangy dipping sauce. Dip each vegetable into the sauce before you eat it.

For the vegetable
  casserole:
3 medium carrots
4 spring onions
4 baby mushrooms
3 cabbage leaves
145g/5oz. tofu
1 vegetable stock cube
600ml/1pint boiling water
2 teaspoons light soy
  sauce
2 tablespoons soft brown
  sugar

half a teaspoon salt
115g/4oz. rice or udon
  noodles

For the dipping sauce:
2 lemons
6 tablespoons light soy
  sauce
1 tablespoon brown
  sugar

Oven temperature:
170°C/325°F/Gas mark 3

1. Peel the carrots and trim off the ends. Cut them in half, then in half, lengthways. Slice each piece into thin strips.

2. Trim off both ends of the spring onions. Then, cut them into pieces about 2cm/1in. long, cutting them at a slant.

# Sushi

Sushi are a popular snack in Japan. They are small parcels of rice flavoured with rice vinegar, seafood, vegetables and raw fish. They are often wrapped in sheets of dried seaweed called nori. In Japan, you can buy takeaway sushi from cafés called sushi bars.

3. Wipe the mushrooms clean. Then, trim the stems and cut a cross in the top of each one. Turn on the oven.

4. Roll each cabbage leaf into a sausage shape. Slice across each one. This will make thin strips when they unroll.

5. Take the tofu out of its packet and cut it carefully into cubes. Make the cubes about 2cm (1in.) across.

6. Stir the stock cube and boiling water together in a jug. Add the soy sauce, brown sugar and salt.

7. Boil the noodles following the instructions on their packet. Arrange the vegetables and noodles in the dish.

8. Pour the stock over everything, then put the lid on the dish. Bake the casserole for about 45 minutes.

Serve the vegetable casserole with long-grain rice.

Pour the dipping sauce into saucers and put one next to each person's bowl.

9. To make the dipping sauce, cut the lemons in half and squeeze them. Put six tablespoons of juice into a bowl.

10. Mix the soy sauce and brown sugar into the lemon juice. Then, put the sauce into the refrigerator to chill.

# Australia

The landscape of Australia is spectacular and very varied. It has sun-baked red deserts in the Outback, tropical rainforests in the north, fine white beaches around its coasts and dry bushlands scattered with eucalyptus trees. Australian recipes include lots of the fresh ingredients found there: tropical fruits, seafood, vegetables, beef and lamb. The cooking is a mixture of European, Asian, Chinese and Japanese.

These are macadamia nuts. They grow in tropical areas of Australia.

The shells of macadamia nuts are incredibly hard to break.

## Lamingtons

These coconut and chocolate sponge cakes are based on a recipe which is very popular in Australia.

225g/8oz. softened butter
175g/6oz. caster sugar
2 eggs
6 tablespoons milk
1 teaspoon vanilla essence or extract
225g/8oz. self-raising flour

For the icing: 115g/4oz. icing sugar
1 tablespoon cocoa powder
2 tablespoons warm water
30g/1oz. desiccated coconut

a baking tray 18x28cm (7x11in.)

Oven temperature:170°C/325°F/Gas mark 3

1. Put the butter and sugar in a bowl. Beat them together with a wooden spoon until thick and creamy.

2. Beat the eggs, then add them to the butter mixture bit by bit. Stir in the milk and vanilla essence or extract.

3. Sift the flour into a bowl. Fold it gently into the cake mixture with a metal spoon. Do not beat it.

4. Grease and line the baking tray. Pour in the mixture and smooth the top with a knife.

Ayers Rock, or Uluru, is a huge rock which stands 348m (1140ft.) high. It is made from sandstone, which appears to change colour at different times of the day.

Traditional Lamingtons are cube-shaped and completely coated in chocolate.

Lamingtons are best eaten the day that you make them.

5. Bake the cake for 25-30 minutes, until it is golden brown. Take it out of the oven and let it cool a little.

6. Cut the cake into 7cm (3in.) squares. Use a spatula to lift them onto a wire rack. Leave them to cool.

7. Sift the icing sugar and cocoa powder into a small bowl. Add the water, to make smooth, runny icing.

8. Spread icing onto the top of each square, letting it run down the sides. Sprinkle a little coconut over each one.

## Internet links

Go to **www.usborne-quicklinks.com** and enter the keywords "world cookbook" for links to the following websites:

**Website 1** Find out lots about the different types of food found in the Australian bush.

**Website 2** Read all about the rich variety of Australian food.

# Internet links

Throughout this book, we have suggested interesting websites where you can find out more about food. To visit the sites, go to the **Usborne Quicklinks Website** at **www.usborne-quicklinks.com** and type the keywords "world cookbook". There you will find links to click on to take you to all the sites, and copies of all the recipes in this book that you can print out and keep.

## Internet safety guidelines

When using the Internet, please make sure you follow these guidelines:

• Ask your parent's or guardian's permission before you connect to the Internet.
• If you write a message in a website guest book or on a website message board, do not include any personal information such as your full name, address or telephone number, and ask an adult before you give your email address.
• If a website asks you to log in or register by typing your name or email address, ask permission of an adult first.
• If you do receive an email from someone you don't know, tell an adult and do not reply to the email.
• Never arrange to meet anyone you have talked to on the Internet.

## Internet help

For general help and advice on using the Internet, go to Usborne Quicklinks at **www.usborne-quicklinks.com** and click on "Net Help". To find out more about how to use your web browser, click on "Help" at the top of the browser, and then choose "Contents and Index". You'll find a huge searchable dictionary containing tips on how to find your way around the Internet easily.

## What you need

The websites described in this book can be accessed using a standard home computer and a web browser (the software that enables you to display information from the Internet). Some sites need additional free programs called "plug-ins" to enable you to watch videos, hear sounds or play interactive games. If you do not have the correct plug-in when you visit those sites, a message will usually appear on your screen with a button to click on to download the plug-in. For more information about plug-ins, go to Usborne Quicklinks and click on "Net Help".

## Site availability

The links in Usborne Quicklinks are regularly reviewed and updated, but occasionally you may get a message that a site is unavailable. This might be temporary, so try again later, or even the next day. If any of the sites close down, we will, if possible, replace them with suitable alternatives, so you will always find an up-to-date list of sites in Usborne Quicklinks.

## Notes for parents and guardians

The websites described in this book are regularly reviewed and the links in Usborne Quicklinks are updated. However, the content of a website may change at any time and Usborne Publishing is not responsible for the content on any website other than its own. We recommend that children are supervised while on the Internet, that they do not use Internet chat rooms, and that you use Internet filtering software to block unsuitable material. Please ensure that your children read and follow the safety guidelines printed on the left. For more information, see the "Net Help" area on the Usborne Quicklinks Website.

# Acknowledgements

Every effort has been made to trace the copyright holders of the material in this book. If any rights have been omitted, the publishers offer to rectify this in any subsequent edition, following notification. The publishers are grateful to the following organizations and individuals for their contributions and permission to reproduce material:

**p.4** Statue of Liberty - ©Gail Mooney/CORBIS; **p.5** New York delicatessen - ©Robert Holmes/CORBIS; **p7** Pumpkins - ©Kevin R. Morris/CORBIS; **p.10** Maple leaves - Digital Vision; Tapping sugar from sap - ©Dr. Scott Nielsen/Bruce Coleman Collection; **p.11** Lake Herbert - ©Erwin and Peggy Bauer/Bruce Coleman Collection; **p.12** Mexican cook - ©Danny Lehman/CORBIS; **p.19**; Caribbean scene - ©Danny Lehman/CORBIS; Fishermen - ©Richard Bickel/CORBIS; **p.21** Harvesting bananas - ©Gary Braasch/CORBIS; **p.23** Ethiopian woman cooking injera - ©Jim Sugar/CORBIS; **p.25** African women pounding grain - ©Penny Tweedie/CORBIS; **p.28** Onions and garlic - ©Michael Busselle/CORBIS; Orchard - ©Eric Crichton/CORBIS; **p.31** French market - ©Michael Busselle/CORBIS; **p.32** Oranges on a tree - ©Ed Young/CORBIS; Handpicking saffron - ©Sandro Prato/Bruce Coleman Collection; **p.36** Pasta shop - Stef Lumley; **p.39** Italian delicatessen - Stef Lumley; **p.42-43** Village in Cotswolds - ©Adam Woolfitt/CORBIS **p.43** Afternoon tea - ©Adam Woolfitt/CORBIS; **p.44** Farmland in Ireland - ©Bruce Coleman inc./Bruce Coleman Collection; **p.46** Three Windmills, the Netherlands - ©Rosemary Calvert/Bruce Coleman Collection; Small Dutch pancakes - ©Owen Franken/CORBIS; **p.49** Christmas market - ©Harald Lange/Bruce Coleman Collection; **p.51** Cake shop in Vienna - ©Adam Woolfitt/CORBIS; **p.53** Swiss cows - ©Hans Reinhard/Bruce Coleman Collection; **p.56** Red peppers and garlic - ©Adam Woolfitt/CORBIS; **p.58** Reindeer - ©Steve Austin; Papilio/CORBIS; **p.61** Swedish coastline - ©Tore Hagman/Bruce Coleman Collection; **p.63** Danish harbour - ©Philip Gould/CORBIS; **p.64** St. Basil's Cathedral - ©Ric Ergenbright/CORBIS; **p.65** Caviar - ©Mark L. Stephenson/CORBIS; **p.66** Egyptian bakers - ©Dave Bartruff/CORBIS; **p.68-69** Olive trees - ©Dave G. Houser/CORBIS; **p.71** Turkish urns - ©Karen Huntt Mason/CORBIS; **p.72** Date palm - ©Hans Reinhard/Bruce Coleman Collection; **p.73** Bowls of spices - ©Dave Bartruff/CORBIS; **p.75** Mezze - © Ludovic Maisant/CORBIS; **p.78** Taj Mahal - ©Jim Zuckerman/CORBIS; Indian vegetable stall - ©Jeremy Homer/CORBIS; **p.82** Floating market in Thailand - ©James Marshall/CORBIS; **p.84** Cloves drying in sun - ©Gerald S. Cubitt/Bruce Coleman Collection; **p.85** Bags at spice market - ©Adam Woolfitt/CORBIS; **p.86** Man weeding a paddy field - ©Jack Fields/CORBIS; **p.90** Rice grains on a stalk - ©Ric Ergenbright/CORBIS; **p.92** Macadamia nuts on a tree - ©Eric and David Hosking/CORBIS;**p.92-93** Ayers Rock - ©Paul A. Souders/ CORBIS; **Endpapers** ©Digital Vision

With thanks also to Rebecca Gilpin, to Non Figg, Vicki Groombridge and Lucy Parris for additional design work, and to Brian Voakes, Mike Olley and Roger Bolton for additional image manipulation.

# Index

This edition first published in 2004 by Usborne Publishing Ltd., Usborne House, 83-85 Saffron Hill, London EC1N 8RT, England. www.usborne.com Copyright © 2004, 2000 Usborne Publishing Ltd. The name Usborne and the devices ⊋ ⊜ are Trade Marks of Usborne Publishing Ltd. All rights reserved. No part of this publication may be reproduced, stored in a retrieval system or transmitted in any form or by any means, electronic, mechanical, photocopying, recording or otherwise without the prior permission of the publisher. Printed in Dubai

CANADA

3
4
5
6
8

12

UNITED STATES
OF AMERICA

ATLANTIC
OCEAN

THE CARIBBEAN

PACIFIC OCEAN

LATIN AMERICA

Key to the numbers

1. NORWAY
2. SWEDEN
3. IRELAND
4. ENGLAND
5. DENMARK
6. HOLLAND
7. GERMANY

8. FRANCE
9. SWITZERLAND
10. AUSTRIA
11. HUNGARY
12. SPAIN
13. ITALY
14. GREECE

This map shows where the
recipes in this book come from.